Solve all your Year 5 Maths problems with CGP!

There's lots to learn in the Year 5 Maths Programme of Study.
Luckily, this fabulous CGP book covers everything pupils need to know.

It's jam-packed with crystal-clear study notes and step-by-step examples — all
perfectly matched to the National Curriculum. We've also included practice
questions for each section to check how much they've understood.

On top of that, you'll also find Greater Depth Questions, so pupils can really test their
knowledge, plus answers to every question. All in all it adds up to Year 5 Maths success!

What CGP is all about

Our sole aim here at CGP is to produce the highest quality
books — carefully written, immaculately presented and
dangerously close to being funny.

Then we work our socks off to get them out to you
— at the cheapest possible prices.

Contents

Section Four — Measurement

Section Five — Geometry

Section Six — Statistics

Published by CGP

Editors:
Martha Bozic, Mary Falkner, Katie Fernandez, Josie Gilbert,
Ali Palin, Camilla Sheridan, Tamara Sinivassen.

ISBN: 978 1 84762 192 4

With thanks to Alison Griffin and Glenn Rogers for the proofreading.
With thanks to Lottie Edwards for the copyright research.

Contains public sector information licensed under the Open Government Licence v3.0.
http://www.nationalarchives.gov.uk/doc/open-government-licence/version/3/

Pages 3, 20 and 26 © Crown Copyright 2020. Contains public sector information licensed
under the Open Government Licence v3.0 - https://www.nationalarchives.gov.uk/doc/
open-government-licence/version/3/

Printed by Elanders Ltd, Newcastle upon Tyne.
Clipart from Corel®
Based on the classic CGP style created by Richard Parsons.

About This Book

This Book has All the Topics for Year 5

By the end of Year 5, you should be able to do all the maths in this book. Each page covers a different topic, with examples to help explain the maths.

This book covers the Attainment Targets for Year 5 of the National Curriculum.

You'll find Greater Depth questions on some pages in boxes like this. Answering these questions will show you've really understood the topic.

 Greater Depth In May, the shop 'Computer Hero' sold 20 000 computers to the nearest ten thousand. In June, they sold 25 000 computers to the nearest thousand. Jia says Computer Hero sold more computers in June. Is she correct? Explain your answer.

At the end of each section are practice questions. You can see what you know and what you don't know.

Some of these are Greater Depth questions — they are marked up with this stamp.

This Study Book has a matching Question Book. It's got questions on all the topics and some practice tests too.

There are Learning Objectives on All Pages

Learning objectives say what you should be able to do. Each learning objective has a set of tick boxes. Tick the one that matches how confident you feel — this will help you work out which bits of Year 5 maths you need more practice with.

I can win gold at the Olympics.

You can use the tick boxes for ongoing assessment to record which attainment targets have been met. A printable checklist of all the Year 5 Learning Objectives can be found at cgpbooks.co.uk/PrimaryMathsLO.

Tick this box if you can do all the maths on the page.

Tick here if you think you need a bit more practice.

If you're really struggling, tick here.

"I can round decimals with two decimal places to the nearest whole number or to one decimal place."

Counting Backwards Through Zero

Adding and Subtracting Negative Numbers

Number lines are really useful for problems using <u>negative numbers</u>.

EXAMPLES: a) What is −5 + 6?

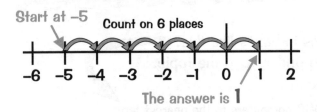

Start at −5   Count on 6 places

−6 −5 −4 −3 −2 −1 0 1 2

The answer is **1**

b) Work out −4 − 13.

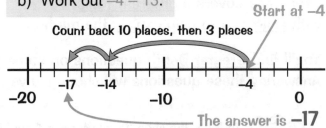

Count back 10 places, then 3 places   Start at −4

−20   −17 −14   −10   −4   0

The answer is **−17**

c) The temperature in my garden this morning is <u>2 °C</u>.
Last night it was <u>8 °C colder</u>. What was the temperature last night?

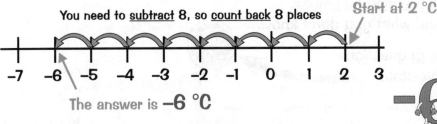

You need to <u>subtract 8</u>, so <u>count back</u> 8 places   Start at 2 °C

−7 −6 −5 −4 −3 −2 −1 0 1 2 3

The answer is **−6 °C**

They're going to get it wrong. I just know it.

Don't be so negative.

Working Out Differences

EXAMPLE:

The temperature in Neil's freezer was −9 °C.
Neil filled his freezer with shoes.
The temperature rose to 2 °C. What was the <u>rise</u> in temperature?

Sketch the number line. Mark the two temperatures on it then <u>count how many degrees</u> there are between them.

It's often easiest to count the places <u>to zero</u>, then the number of places <u>after zero</u>, and then add them together... 9 + 2 = <u>11 °C</u>.

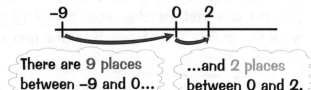

−9   0 2

There are 9 places between −9 and 0...   ...and 2 places between 0 and 2.

EXAMPLE:

The temperature in Icetown is <u>−46 °C</u>.
The temperature in Froston is <u>−12 °C</u>.
Find the <u>difference</u> between these temperatures.

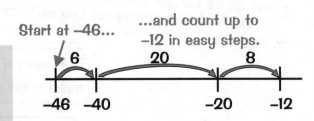

Start at −46...   ...and count up to −12 in easy steps.

6   20   8

−46 −40   −20   −12

So the difference is 6 + 20 + 8 = <u>34 °C</u>.
(You could also do this by counting back from −12 to −46.)

"I can count backwards and forwards through zero, and solve problems with negative numbers in."

 ✓ ✓ ✓

Place Value in Big Numbers

7-digit Numbers are into the Millions

Look at this whopping number — the digit furthest to the left is the <u>millions</u>:

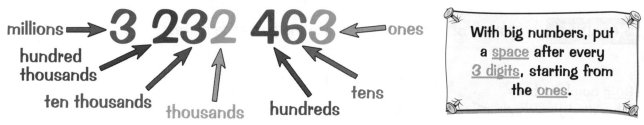

millions → **3 232 463** ← ones
hundred thousands
ten thousands
thousands
hundreds
tens

> With big numbers, put a <u>space</u> after every <u>3 digits</u>, starting from the <u>ones</u>.

So, it's:
"Three million, two hundred and thirty-two thousand, four hundred and sixty-three."

EXAMPLE: Write out in numbers: Two <u>million</u>, one hundred and sixty-one <u>thousand</u>, nine <u>hundred</u> and twenty-four.

two million → **2 161 924**
one hundred and sixty-one thousand
nine hundred and twenty-four

Big Numbers Can Be Partitioned

The number **235 896** can be partitioned into
<u>2 hundred thousands</u>, <u>3 ten thousands</u>, <u>5 thousands</u>, <u>8 hundreds</u>, <u>9 tens</u> and <u>6 ones</u>.

There aren't any millions.

M	HTh	TTh	Th	H	T	O
	2	3	5	8	9	6

So 235 896 = 200 000 + 30 000 + 5000 + 800 + 90 + 6.

You can partition a number in lots of different ways. For example...

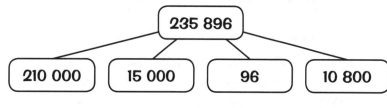

235 896
210 000 | 15 000 | 96 | 10 800

Greater Depth 752 163 = 700 000 + 50 000 + 2000 + 100 + 60 + 3
Can you think of 3 other ways to partition 752 163?

"I can read, write and partition numbers up to a million." ✓ ✓ ✓

Ordering and Comparing Big Numbers

Big Numbers Can Be Compared

The < symbol means "is less than", and > means "is greater than".

EXAMPLE: Put a < or > in the box to make the sentence correct.

786 451 ☐ 785 989

Both numbers have 7 hundred thousands.

Both have 8 ten thousands.

The left number has 6 thousands, but the right number only has 5. So you need to put > in the box to show the left number is bigger.

Answer: 786 451 > 785 989

Big Numbers Can Be Ordered Too

EXAMPLES: Put these numbers in ascending order:
21 542, 22 687, 16 548, 2467

Ascending means going up (from smallest to largest).

2467   16 548   22 687   21 542

This is smallest. It's got no ten thousands.

This is next smallest. It's got fewer ten thousands than 21 542 or 22 687.

Now compare 21 542 and 22 687. Which is smaller? They both have 2 ten thousands. So look at the thousands. 21 542 is smaller than 22 687.

So the right order is: 2467, 16 548, 21 542, 22 687.

Put these lottery prizes in ascending order.
£4 382 596, £3 427 508, £95 456, £4 378 490, £448 670.

£95 456
£448 670
£3 427 508
£4 378 490
£4 382 596

Starting with the smallest, write the amounts one below the other — it's easier to check your answer.

"I can compare numbers up to a million and put them in order of size."

Section One — Number and Place Value

Counting in Powers of 10

One Followed by Just Zeros is a Power of 10

These numbers are all <u>powers of 10</u>:

| 10 | 100 | 1000 | 10 000 | 100 000 | 1 000 000 |

Counting On in Powers of 10

This means <u>adding on</u> 10, or 1000, or 10 000, or another power of 10, <u>each time</u>.

EXAMPLE: From 618 950, <u>count on</u> in steps of 100 000. Stop at 918 950.

To count up in 100 000s you need to add 100 000 each time. To do this, just <u>add 1</u> to the <u>hundred thousands</u> digit each time. So, find the <u>hundred thousands digit</u>. Here, it's the 6. 618 950

Add 1 to this digit each time: 618 950   718 950   818 950   918 950
add 1   add 1   add 1

EXAMPLE: From 0, <u>count on</u> in steps of 1 000 000. Stop at 4 000 000.

You're starting at zero, and adding 1 million each time, so add 1 to the millions digit:

0   1 000 000   2 000 000   3 000 000   4 000 000
add 1   add 1   add 1   add 1

Counting Back in Powers of 10

This means <u>subtracting</u> a power of 10 <u>each time</u>.

EXAMPLE: <u>Count down</u> from 152 068 in steps of 10 000. Stop after two steps.

To count down in steps of 10 000 you need to <u>subtract</u> 10 000 each time. To do this, just <u>take 1 away</u> from the <u>ten thousands</u> digit each time.

The <u>ten thousands</u> digit is the 5.   152 068   142 068   132 068
subtract 1   subtract 1

"I can count forwards or backwards in thousands, tens of thousands, hundreds of thousands, or millions."

Rounding

Rounding Whole Numbers

This is quite easy if you remember the RULES:

The Rounding Rules

1. The number lies between two possible answers. You have to decide which one it's nearer to.
2. Look at the digit to the right of the place you're rounding to — the DECIDER.
3. If the decider is 5 or more then round UP. If the decider is less than 5 then round DOWN.

Th	H	T	O
4	8	5	6

For example, if you round to the nearest Hundred, the decider is the Tens digit — here it's a 5.

EXAMPLE:
Last year, 23 superheroes turned into computers. How many is 23 to the nearest ten?

23 is between 20 and 30.
The decider is 3 so round down to 20.

EXAMPLE:
A superhero flew into 1851 windows in one year. How many is 1851 to the nearest thousand?

1851 is between 1000 and 2000.
The decider is 8 so round up to 2000.
(On a number line, you can see it's closer to 2000.)

1000 — 1500 — 2000

EXAMPLE:
Last year, 450 029 computers dreamed they were superheroes. How many is 450 029 to the nearest hundred thousand?

450 029 is between 400 000 and 500 000.
The decider is 5 so round up to 500 000.

 Greater Depth In May, the shop 'Computer Hero' sold 20 000 computers to the nearest ten thousand. In June, they sold 25 000 computers to the nearest thousand. Jia says Computer Hero sold more computers in June. Is she correct? Explain your answer.

"I can round to the nearest 10, 100, 1000, 10 000 or 100 000."

Roman Numerals

The Romans Used Numerals Instead of Digits

The Romans used <u>letters</u> called <u>numerals</u> instead of the <u>digits 0-9</u>.
You need to know <u>these</u> numerals:

$$I = 1 \quad X = 10 \quad C = 100 \quad M = 1000$$
$$V = 5 \quad L = 50 \quad D = 500$$

For <u>other</u> numbers, they put <u>numerals in a row</u>.
Here are the <u>rules</u> you need to read them:

Numerals that are <u>the same</u> are <u>added together</u>. → II = **2**   XX = **20**   CCC = **300**

<u>Small</u> numerals <u>after</u> big ones are <u>added on</u> to the big one. → XI = **11**   CII = **102**   CCCXX = **320**

<u>Small</u> numerals <u>before</u> big ones are <u>subtracted</u> from the big one.
(These six are the only subtractions allowed.) → IV = **4**   XL = **40**   CD = **400**
IX = **9**   XC = **90**   CM = **900**

Do any <u>subtracting</u> <u>before</u> doing any <u>adding</u>.

CXC = 190
100
100 − 10 = 90

XXIX = 29
10 + 10 = 20
10 − 1 = 9

CXCV = 195
100   5
100 − 10 = 90

You Can Write Years in Roman Numerals

<u>2000</u> is written <u>MM</u>
so years in the 2000s will begin MM

MMXIV = 2014

<u>1900</u> is written <u>MCM</u>
so years in the 1900s will begin MCM

MCMLXXIX = 1979

<u>1800</u> is written <u>MDCCC</u>
so years in the 1800s will begin MDCCC

MDCCCXLV = 1845

"I can read Roman numerals up to M, and recognise years written in Roman numerals."

Practice Questions

1) Work out:

   a) −3 − 4   b) −2 + 7   c) 6 − 13

2) Write $<$ or $>$ to make these statements correct.

   a) −7 ☐ 4   b) −5 ☐ −9

3) Round 845 327:

   a) to the nearest hundred thousand.

   b) to the nearest thousand.

   c) to the nearest ten.

4) What is the value of each of these digits in 4 215 367?

   a) 4   b) 2   c) 5

5) Write out in numbers:

   a) One million, four hundred and forty thousand, five hundred and sixty-three.

   b) Nine hundred and seven thousand, two hundred and forty-four.

6) Put the numbers below in order from smallest to largest.

   22 100   22 567   23 176   22 504

7) Fill in the gaps in the sequence by counting down from 53 259 in steps of 1000.

   53 259   ☐   ☐   ☐   49 259

Section One — Number and Place Value

Practice Questions

8) The temperature in the penguin house is 3 °C. The penguins are happy at –6 °C. What change in temperature is needed to make the penguins happy?

9) The temperature in Barrow, Alaska is –18 °C.
The temperature in Barrow-in-Furness, Cumbria is 15 °C warmer.

    a) What is the temperature in Barrow-in-Furness?

    b) What is 15 °C rounded to the nearest 10 °C?

10) What number is shown by the Roman numeral DLXX?

11) In the Bakershire elections, the Ice Cream Party got 564 625 votes.

    a) The Cheese Party got 563 968 votes.
       Who got more votes — the Cheese Party or the Ice Cream Party?

    b) Round 564 625 to the nearest thousand.

    c) Round 563 968 to the nearest ten thousand.

12) What year is shown by the Roman numeral MCMXCI?

13) Lars has a table showing the population of different places in Roman times.

Place	Population
Brigantum	MMMDCXXXVII
Roundle	MMMCDLXVII
Hillsius	MMCMXLIX
Ulverstiun	MMMCDXXIV

    a) Write the population of Roundle in numbers.

    b) Write the population pf Brigantum in numbers, rounded to the nearest 100.

    c) Write the places in order from smallest to largest population.

Written Adding

You Can Add in Columns

EXAMPLE: Work out 54 653 + 21 694

```
  TTh Th H T O
    5 4 6 5 3
+   2 1 6 9 4
            7
```

First, write the numbers on top of each other with the ones lined up.

1 Add the ones column first.

```
  TTh Th H T O
    5 4 6 5 3
+   2 1 6 9 4
            7
```
3 + 4 = 7

2 Add the tens column next...

5 + 9 = 14

```
  TTh Th H T O
    5 4 6 5 3
+   2 1 6 9 4
          4 7
          1
```

The 4 goes in the tens answer space...

10 tens = 100.
So carry 100 to the hundreds column.

3 ...then the hundreds.

6 + 6 + 1 = 13

```
  TTh Th H T O
    5 4 6 5 3
+   2 1 6 9 4
        3 4 7
        1 1
```

3 goes in the hundreds column...

10 hundreds = 1000.
So carry 1000 to the thousands column.

4 Add the thousands and ten thousands.

5 + 2 = 7

4 + 1 + 1 = 6

```
  TTh Th H T O
    5 4 6 5 3
+   2 1 6 9 4
    7 6 3 4 7
      1 1
```

So 54 653 + 21 694 = 76 347

Add Decimals the Same Way

EXAMPLE: Work out 42.85 + 16.74

When you write the numbers down, always line up the decimal points. Then start adding, beginning with the place value column of least value (it's always on the right).

1 Add the hundredths.

```
  T O . t h
  4 2 . 8 5
+ 1 6 . 7 4
      .   9
```
5 + 4 = 9

Always put the decimal point in first.

2 Add the tenths.

8 + 7 = 15

```
  T O . t h
  4 2 . 8 5
+ 1 6 . 7 4
      . 5 9
        1
```

The 5 goes in the tenths answer space...

10 tenths = 1.
So carry 1 to the ones column.

3 Add the ones.

2 + 6 + 1 = 9

```
  T O . t h
  4 2 . 8 5
+ 1 6 . 7 4
    9 . 5 9
    1
```

Remember to add this 1 too.

4 Add the tens.

```
  T O . t h
  4 2 . 8 5
+ 1 6 . 7 4
  5 9 . 5 9
  1
```

4 + 1 = 5

So 42.85 + 16.74 = 59.59
(Don't forget the decimal point.)

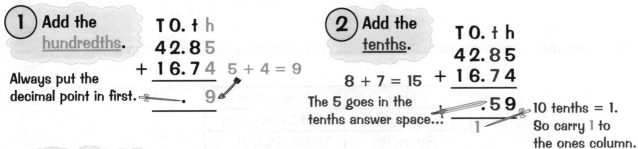
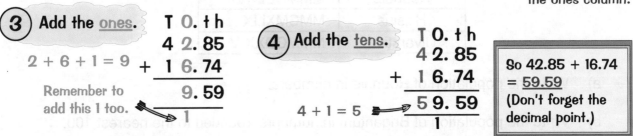

"I can use standard written methods to add numbers."

Written Subtracting

In Subtractions, You May Need to Exchange

You set out subtractions the same as additions. Line up the ones or decimal points.
Then you start subtracting with the column of least place value.

EXAMPLE: What is 32 834 – 11 216?

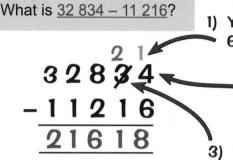

$$\begin{array}{r} {\scriptstyle 2\ 1} \\ 3\ 2\ 8\ \cancel{3}\ 4 \\ -\ 1\ 1\ 2\ 1\ 6 \\ \hline 2\ 1\ 6\ 1\ 8 \end{array}$$

1) You can't do 4 – 6 because 6 is bigger than 4.

2) But you can exchange a ten from the 30 for 10 ones. Add those 10 ones onto the 4 to make 14.
Then 14 – 6 = 8.

3) There's 10 less here because you changed a ten into ones.

Subtracting in Columns

EXAMPLE: Work out 382.1 – 129.6.

(1) Line up the decimal points.

$$\begin{array}{r} H\ T\ O.t \\ 3\ 8\ 2.1 \\ -\ 1\ 2\ 9.6 \\ \hline . \end{array}$$

(2) Subtract the **TENTHS**.
You can't do 1 – 6, so exchange one of the ones for 10 tenths.
Then 11 – 6 = 5.

$$\begin{array}{r} H\ T\ O.t \\ {\scriptstyle 1\ 1} \\ 3\ 8\ \cancel{2}.1 \\ -\ 1\ 2\ 9.6 \\ \hline .5 \end{array}$$

(3) Subtract the **ONES**.
You can't do 1 – 9, so exchange a ten for 10 ones.
Then 11 – 9 = 2.

$$\begin{array}{r} H\ T\ O.t \\ {\scriptstyle 7\ 11\ 1} \\ 3\ \cancel{8}\ \cancel{2}.1 \\ -\ 1\ 2\ 9.6 \\ \hline 2.5 \end{array}$$

(4) Subtract the **TENS**.
7 – 2 = 5

$$\begin{array}{r} H\ T\ O.t \\ {\scriptstyle 7\ 11\ 1} \\ 3\ \cancel{8}\ \cancel{2}.1 \\ -\ 1\ 2\ 9.6 \\ \hline 5\ 2.5 \end{array}$$

(5) Subtract the **HUNDREDS**.
3 – 1 = 2

$$\begin{array}{r} H\ T\ O.t \\ {\scriptstyle 7\ 11\ 1} \\ 3\ \cancel{8}\ \cancel{2}.1 \\ -\ 1\ 2\ 9.6 \\ \hline 2\ 5\ 2.5 \end{array}$$

Subtracting from a number with zeros in is a bit harder.

You can't do 3 – 6 in the ones column, but there are no tens to exchange for 10 ones...

... so exchange a hundred for 10 tens.

Then exchange a ten for 10 ones. So you have 9 tens left.

Now you have 13 ones so you can subtract.
13 – 6 = 7

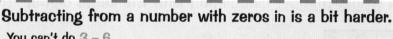
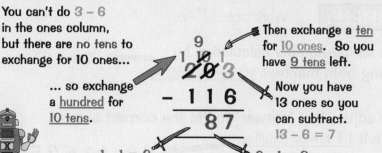

1 – 1 = 0   9 – 1 = 8

"I can use standard written methods to subtract numbers."

Mental Adding and Subtracting

Adding and Subtracting in Your Head

There are some <u>tricks</u> you can use to make adding and subtracting in your head easier.

Partition Numbers into Thousands, Hundreds, Tens and Ones

EXAMPLES:

What is 13 157 + 8600?

13 157 + 8600

13 000 + 8000 + 100 + 600 + 57

21 000 + 700 + 57 = <u>21 757</u>

What is 9200 – 6700?

> Start subtracting with the <u>thousands</u>, then the <u>hundreds</u>.

9200 – 6700
= 9200 – 6000 – 700
= 3200 – 700
= <u>2500</u>

Addition and Subtraction are Inverses

Inverse just means <u>opposite</u>. For any addition you can think of, there is always a <u>matching subtraction</u>. And every subtraction has a <u>matching addition</u>.

EXAMPLE:

$57 + 86 = 143$

so you also know that $\quad 143 - 86 = 57$

and $\quad 143 - 57 = 86$

So you can make <u>lots</u> of number sentences from just <u>one</u> piece of information.

Adding and Subtracting Decimals in Your Head

Once you can add and subtract whole numbers, decimals are easy.
Do a <u>whole-number</u> calculation with the same digits. Then <u>adjust</u> the answer.

EXAMPLE: Work out 9.2 – 6.7

Do a whole-number calculation by making both numbers <u>10 times bigger</u>. → $92 - 67 = 25$

Now adjust that 'answer' to get the correct answer.
Make it <u>10 times smaller</u>. → $9.2 - 6.7 = \underline{2.5}$

From $92 - 67 = 25$,
you also know that:
$0.92 - 0.67 = 0.25$
$0.67 + 0.25 = 0.92$
$6.7 + 2.5 = 9.2$ ...etc...

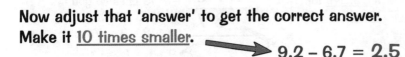

"I can add and subtract numbers mentally."

Rounding and Checking

Round Numbers to Estimate Answers

If you need to make a quick estimate, a good way to do it is by rounding.

EXAMPLE: Estimate: 41.37 + 21.08

To do a quick estimation, round each number to the nearest ten: **40 + 20 = 60**

Or you could round to the nearest whole number.

41 and 21 are nearer the 'real' numbers than 40 and 20. So this is a better estimate. **41 + 21 = 62**

Both 'real numbers' were bigger. So the real answer should be a bit more than 62.

Use Inverses to Check Calculations

One way to check an answer is to do the inverse calculation. You should get back to the number you started with. Remember:

ADDITION and SUBTRACTION are inverses.

MULTIPLICATION and DIVISION are inverses.

EXAMPLE: What is 6.3 − 4.5?

Step 1) DO IT: 6.3 − 4.5 = 1.8
Step 2) CHECK IT: 1.8 + 4.5 = 6.3 ✓

EXAMPLE: What is 72 ÷ 6?

Step 1) DO IT: 72 ÷ 6 = 12
Step 2) CHECK IT: 12 × 6 = 72 ✓

Always Check that Your Answer is Sensible

It's easy to make mistakes. Always read your answer and see if it makes sense.

"The penguin is 1 m tall." ← This is OK.

"The book is 2 m high." ← This can't be right. You don't get 2 metre high books.

Greater Depth
Luis is playing a game. He adds 762 points to his starting score, but then loses 438 points. He is now on 467 points. He estimates his starting score by doing inverse calculations with all of the numbers rounded to the nearest ten. Will his estimated score be more or less than his real score? Explain your answer.

"I can round numbers to check my answers, and I can check that my answers are sensible."

Square and Cube Numbers

Square Numbers

When you multiply a number by itself, you get a <u>square number</u>.
Here are the first few square numbers:

1	4	9	16	25	36	49	64	81	100	121	144...
(1×1)	(2×2)	(3×3)	(4×4)	(5×5)	(6×6)	(7×7)	(8×8)	(9×9)	(10×10)	(11×11)	(12×12)...

They're called <u>square numbers</u> because they are the areas in this pattern of squares.

$1 \times 1 = 1$

$2 \times 2 = 4$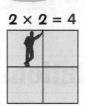

$3 \times 3 = 9$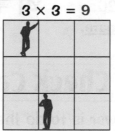

$4 \times 4 = 16$

There's a quick way to write them.
You write <u>five squared</u> as 5^2.

EXAMPLES:
a) $7^2 = 7 \text{ squared} = 7 \times 7 = \mathbf{49}.$
b) $15^2 = 15 \text{ squared} = 15 \times 15 = \mathbf{225}.$

Cube Numbers

You get a cube number by multiplying a number by itself <u>twice</u>.

EXAMPLES:
3 cubed = $3 \times 3 \times 3 = \mathbf{27}.$
5 cubed = $5 \times 5 \times 5 = \mathbf{125}.$

They're called <u>cube numbers</u> because they are the volumes in this pattern of cubes:

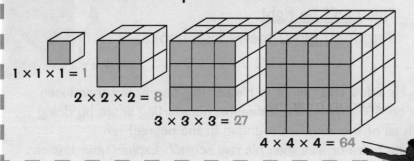

$1 \times 1 \times 1 = 1$
$2 \times 2 \times 2 = 8$
$3 \times 3 \times 3 = 27$
$4 \times 4 \times 4 = 64$

The quick way to write
four cubed is $\underline{4^3}$.

"I can recognise and use square and cube numbers."

Multiples

Multiples are Just Like Times Tables

So the <u>multiples of 2</u> are just the numbers in the <u>2 times table</u>:

2   4   6   8   10   12   14   16   ...

The <u>multiples of 8</u> are   8   16   24   32   40   48   ...

The <u>multiples of 12</u> are   12   24   36   48   60   72   84   ...

> It's easy to remember: MULTIPLes are just MULTIPLication tables.

The Last Digit Helps You Spot Multiples

Some multiples are easy to spot.

<u>Multiples of 10</u> all end in <u>0</u>.

<u>Multiples of 5</u> all end in <u>0</u> or <u>5</u>.

<u>Multiples of 4</u> can be <u>halved</u> and <u>halved again</u> to give a <u>whole number</u>.

<u>Multiples of 2</u> all end in <u>even numbers</u> or <u>0</u>.

EXAMPLES:

a) **50** <u>ends in zero</u>, so it's a multiple of 2, a multiple of 5 and a multiple of 10.

b) **175** <u>ends in five</u>, so it's a multiple of 5.

c) **364** <u>ends in four</u>, so it's a multiple of 2.

Finding Common Multiples

A <u>common multiple</u> of two numbers is a number that's a <u>multiple of both numbers</u>. You can find them by <u>listing times tables</u>.

EXAMPLE: Find a <u>common multiple</u> of 6 and 8.

1) Write out the <u>6 times table</u>...
(Go up to 5 × 6 to start with.)   →   6   12   18   24   30

2) ...then the <u>8 times table</u>.   →   8   16   24   ...

3) Look out for a number that's <u>in both lists</u>. When you find one, it's a common multiple. (There are lots, but you only need one for this question, so stop here.)

So a common multiple of 6 and 8 is <u>24</u>.

"I can identify multiples of numbers."   ✓ ✓ ✓

Factors and Primes

Factors of a Number

The <u>factors</u> of a number are whole numbers that <u>divide exactly into</u> that number.

EXAMPLES:

The number 10 has factors 1, 10, 2 and 5
because $1 \times 10 = 10$ and $2 \times 5 = 10$

The number 12 has factors 1, 12, 2, 6, 3 and 4
because $1 \times 12 = 12$, $2 \times 6 = 12$ and $3 \times 4 = 12$

1 and 2 are <u>common factors</u> of 10 and 12.

That means 10 and 12 <u>share</u> the factors 1 and 2.

A number is <u>divisible</u> (can be divided exactly) by all its factors.

EXAMPLE: Circle the numbers that have 6 as a common factor.

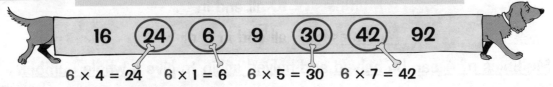

16   (24)   (6)   9   (30)   (42)   92

$6 \times 4 = 24$ $6 \times 1 = 6$ $6 \times 5 = 30$ $6 \times 7 = 42$

Factors Come in Pairs

The <u>smallest factor</u> makes a pair with the <u>biggest one</u>, the <u>second smallest</u> makes a pair with the <u>second biggest</u>, and so on.

EXAMPLE: List the factor pairs of 20.

3 won't multiply by a whole number to make 20.

$1 \times 20 = 20$
$2 \times 10 = 20$
$4 \times 5 = 20$

If you carry on like this, the next one would be 5×4... but that's the same as 4×5, so stop here.

So the factor pairs of 20 are <u>1 and 20</u>, <u>2 and 10</u>, <u>4 and 5</u>.

If there are an <u>odd</u> number of factors, the <u>middle factor</u> multiplies by <u>itself</u>. For example, the factors of 9 are 1, 3 and 9.

$1 \times 9 = 9$
$3 \times 3 = 9$

Prime Numbers Only Have Two Factors

A <u>prime number</u> is a number that has <u>exactly TWO FACTORS</u>: 1 and <u>itself</u>.

1) <u>1 is NOT a prime number</u> — it doesn't have exactly 2 factors.
2) All prime numbers end in <u>1, 3, 7 or 9</u>. <u>2 and 5 are the EXCEPTIONS</u>.
3) <u>2</u> is the only <u>even</u> prime.

BUT <u>not all</u> numbers ending in 1, 3, 7 or 9 are prime. See the next page...

"I can find all the factor pairs of a number and the common factors of two numbers."

Factors and Primes

To Check if a Number is a Prime Number...

1) Does it end in 1, 3, 7 or 9 (or is it 2 or 5)?
2) Does it have any <u>factors</u> apart from itself and 1?
   If it has, it's not a prime.

EXAMPLE: I'm thinking of a prime number. It's more than 80 but less than 85. What is the number?

81 and 83 are the only numbers that end in a <u>1</u> or a <u>3</u>.
But $9 \times 9 = 81$, so it has factors other than itself and 1. So the number must be <u>83</u>.

Here are the prime numbers up to 100.

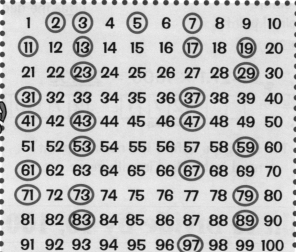

BINGO!

Finding Prime Factors

<u>Whole numbers</u> that <u>aren't prime</u> are made up of <u>prime</u> numbers <u>multiplied together</u>. These numbers are called <u>prime factors</u>.

EXAMPLE: Which prime numbers multiply together to make 56?

All apart from 1.

1) Write down any factor pair of 56. → $56 = 7 \times 8$

2) 7 is a prime number. It is a <u>prime factor</u> of 56. → $56 = 7 \times 2 \times 4$
   8 <u>isn't</u> a prime (it's a <u>composite number</u>), so split it up into a factor pair.

3) 2 is prime. 4 isn't, so split 4 into 2×2. → $56 = \underline{7 \times 2 \times 2 \times 2}$
   Now <u>all</u> the factors are prime.

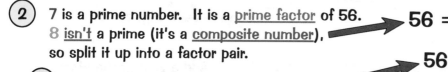

 Greater Depth Mia is 35. How old will she be when her age next shares a prime factor with 35?

"I can spot prime numbers up to 100 and find the prime factors of numbers."

Multiplying and Dividing by 10, 100 and 1000

Move Digits Left to Multiply by 10, 100 or 1000

If you're multiplying by 10, move the digits ONE PLACE to the LEFT.

If you multiply by 100, move the digits TWO PLACES to the LEFT.

The number of zeros tells you the number of places to move.

$35 \times 10 = \underline{350}$

| | 3 | 5 | . |
| | 3 | 5 | 0 | . |

Add a decimal point if there isn't one.

Fill in the empty places before the decimal point with zeros.

Add a zero in here as a placeholder.

$75.9 \times 100 = \underline{7590}$

	7	5	.	9
7	5	9	0	.	0
7	5	9	0

There's no need to add zeros after the decimal point.

To multiply by 1000, move the digits THREE PLACES to the LEFT.

$27.1 \times 1000 = \underline{27\,100}$

		2	7	.	1
2	7	1	0	0	.	0
2	7	1	0	0

The two gaps before the decimal point need to be filled in with zeros.

You don't need a zero here.

Move Digits Right to Divide by 10, 100 or 1000

To divide by 10 move the digits ONE PLACE to the RIGHT.

$8.6 \div 10 = \underline{0.86}$

8	.	6	
	.	8	6
0	.	8	6

You need to put a zero before the decimal point.

You might have to add or remove zeros.

To divide by 100 move the digits TWO PLACES to the RIGHT.

$7.5 \div 100 = \underline{0.075}$

7	.	5		
	.		7	5
0	.	0	7	5

Fill in the gaps with zeros.

To divide by 1000 move the digits THREE PLACES to the RIGHT.

$600 \div 1000 = \underline{0.6}$

6	0	0	.			
			.	6	0	0
		0	.	6	0	0

Add a decimal point.

Add a zero at the start.

You can remove these zeros.

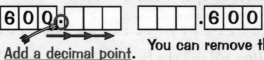

"I can multiply and divide a whole number or decimal by 10, 100 or 1000."

Mental Multiplying

Break Calculations into Steps

It helps to break calculations into simple steps.

EXAMPLE: What is fifty multiplied by four?

You know that 50 × 2 = 100.
So 4 lots of 50 will just be double this.
So 4 × 50 = 200.

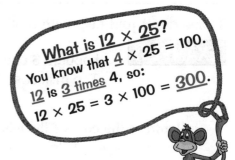

What is 12 × 25?
You know that 4 × 25 = 100.
12 is 3 times 4, so:
12 × 25 = 3 × 100 = 300.

You can use scaling to help with calculations too...

9 × 0.7 = ? → You know that 9 × 7 = 63.
0.7 is one tenth the size of 7, so 9 × 0.7 must be one tenth the size of 9 × 7.

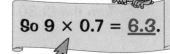

So 9 × 0.7 = 6.3.

Make an Easier Calculation First

It's often easier to do the calculation with a near number first, then adjust it.

EXAMPLE: Stephanie eats 98 woodlice every day. How many woodlice does she eat in six days?

You want to work out 98 × 6. 98 is the same as 100 − 2.
So work out 100 × 6 then subtract 2 × 6.

100 × 6 = 600
2 × 6 = 12

So 98 × 6 = 600 − 12 = 588 woodlice

Because you had an 'extra 2' six times when you did 100 × 6.

EXAMPLE: Bananas cost £1.95 per bunch. How much would 16 bunches cost?

You want to work out £1.95 × 16. A near, easier calculation is £2 × 16.
So work out £2 × 16 then subtract 5p × 16.

16 + 16 = £32

16 is 2 lots of 8.
5p × 8 = 40p.
40p + 40p = 80p

The difference between £1.95 and £2 is 5p, so you had an 'extra 5p' 16 times when you did £2 × 16.

So 16 bunches cost £32 − £0.80 = £31.20

"I can solve problems by multiplying in my head."

Mental Dividing

Your Times Tables are Really Useful

Tables don't just help with multiplying. They help with <u>dividing</u> too.

EXAMPLE: I bought 3 chocolate bars and one carton of milk. I paid £2.40. The milk cost 60p. How much did <u>one chocolate bar</u> cost?

Subtract the cost of the milk from the total.
Do it in stages. 60p = 40p + 20p

£2.40 – 40p = £2
£2 – 20p = <u>£1.80</u>

<u>3 chocolate bars</u> cost £1.80
<u>Divide by 3</u> to find the cost of one.
Turn the £1.80 into 180p first.

You know that 3 × 6 = 18.
So you know that 18 ÷ 3 = 6.
So 180p ÷ 3 = 60p

So one chocolate bar costs <u>60p</u>.

Split Numbers to Make Division Easier

Dividing a number in your head is easier if you break the calculation into <u>steps</u>.
There are <u>two ways</u> you could do this.

(1) You can split the number you're dividing by into a <u>factor pair</u>...

EXAMPLE: What is 80 ÷ 16?

The factors of 16 are 1, (2), 4, (8) and 16.

2 × 8 = 16

So dividing by <u>16</u> is the same as dividing by <u>2 then 8</u> (or by <u>8 then 2</u>).

STEP 1: Divide 80 by 8. 80 ÷ 8 = 10
STEP 2: Divide 10 by 2. 10 ÷ 2 = 5

So 80 ÷ 16 = <u>5</u>

(2) ...or you can <u>partition</u> the larger number.

EXAMPLE: What is 161 ÷ 7?

<u>Partition</u> 161 into numbers that are <u>easy to divide by 7</u>.

161 ÷ 7

140 ÷ 7   21 ÷ 7

140 and 21 are both easy to divide by 7.

You know that 14 ÷ 7 = 2,
so you also know that
140 ÷ 7 = 20

21 ÷ 7 = 3

20 + 3 = 23   So 161 ÷ 7 = <u>23</u>

"I can divide numbers in my head."

Written Multiplication

Long Multiplication

EXAMPLE: What is 1243 × 24?

Do a quick <u>estimation</u> before you start:
1243 × 24 ≈ 1000 × 25 = 25 000

This looks tricky, but it's not.
You're multiplying by a <u>two-digit</u> number.
First, you need to <u>partition</u> this number: 24 = 20 + 4.
Then work out 1243 × 20 and 1243 × 4 <u>separately</u>, and <u>add them together</u>.

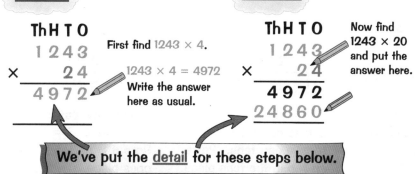

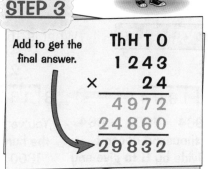

We've put the <u>detail</u> for these steps below.

STEP 1: 1243 × 4

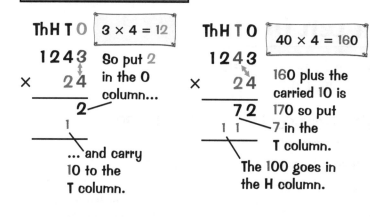

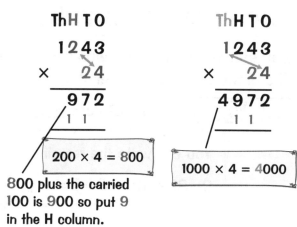

STEP 2: 1243 × 20

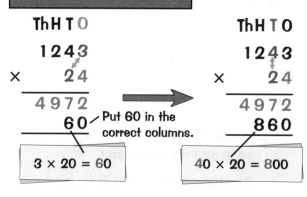

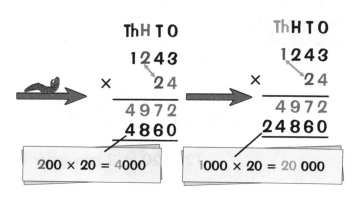

"I can multiply a four-digit number by a two-digit number."

Written Division

Short Division

This method is good for dividing by a <u>one-digit number</u>.

1) <u>Partition</u> the big number into thousands, hundreds, tens and ones. Divide each of these numbers, starting with the <u>highest</u> place value. (It's different from adding, subtracting and multiplying.)

2) Put the <u>result</u> of each division <u>on top</u> in the correct place value column.

3) Sometimes you need to <u>exchange</u>. This example shows you how.

EXAMPLE: What is 1664 ÷ 8?

$$8\overline{)1\,6\,6\,4}$$

1664 = 1000 + 664
1 thousand doesn't divide by 8 to give any thousands, so exchange the 1 thousand for 10 hundreds.

$$\overset{2}{8\overline{)1\,{}^16\,6\,4}}$$

You've got 16 in the hundreds place.
1600 ÷ 8 = 200
So put 2 on top in the hundreds place.

$$\overset{2\,0}{8\overline{)1\,6\,6\,{}^64}}$$

64 = 60 + 4
6 tens don't divide by 8 to give any tens. Put a 0 on top in the tens place. Exchange the 6 tens for 60 ones.

$$\overset{2\,0\,8}{8\overline{)1\,6\,6\,{}^64}}$$

You've now got 64 ones.
64 ÷ 8 = 8
So put 8 on top in the ones place.

So the answer is <u>208</u>.

The Remainder is the Bit Left Over

Sometimes one number won't divide perfectly by another.
The amount <u>left over</u> after the division is called the <u>remainder</u>.

EXAMPLE: 10 into 31 goes <u>3 times with remainder 1</u> (because 3 × 10 = 30)

You can write the remainder as a <u>number</u>, a <u>fraction</u> or a <u>decimal</u>.

So $31 \div 10 = 3 \text{ r } 1 = 3\frac{1}{10} = 3.1$

The number on the bottom of the fraction needs to be the number you were dividing by.

Sometimes you'll need to round the answer to a whole number.

EXAMPLE: Giant worms cost 20p for a bag of 3. Herman has 72p. How many bags of worms can he afford?

You need to know how many 20p's you can get out of 72p.
So it's <u>how many times 20 goes into 72</u>.

72 ÷ 20 = 3 remainder 12.

You can't buy bits of a bag, so <u>ignore</u> the remainder.

So Herman can buy <u>3 bags</u>.

"I can divide a four-digit number by a one-digit number and deal with remainders."

Solving Calculation Problems

Show Word Problems as Calculations

EXAMPLE:

Hansa can dig <u>5 holes</u> in an <u>hour</u>.
How long would it take her to dig <u>20 holes</u>?

You need to <u>DIVIDE</u> the total number of holes
by the number of holes she can dig per hour. ⟹ 20 ÷ 5 = <u>4 hours</u>

EXAMPLE:

Bob is <u>two thirds</u> of the height of Fred.
How tall is Bob if Fred is <u>180 cm</u>?

You know that
18 ÷ 3 = 6

This is <u>one third</u>
of Fred's height.

180 ÷ 3 = 60

Find two thirds of 180. So <u>DIVIDE</u> by 3...

...then <u>MULTIPLY</u> by 2.   60 × 2 = 120

So Bob is <u>120 cm</u> tall.

You know that 6 × 2 = 12

EXAMPLE:

Ashraf works for <u>4 hours</u> and is paid <u>£6 an hour</u>.
Ali earns the <u>same</u> amount in <u>3 hours</u>. How much is Ali paid per hour?

6 × 4 = 3 × ☐   ↦ Show the missing number.

We can put an <u>equals sign</u> in here because we
know that 6 × 4 and 3 × ☐ give the <u>same answer</u>.

6 × 4 = 24
So 24 = 3 × ☐ ⟸ Work out what you need to times 3 by to give 24.
3 × 8 = 24, so Ali is paid <u>£8</u> an hour.

You Can Use Brackets in Calculations

EXAMPLE:

Every day Jane buys 12 carrots and then gives 4 carrots away.
How many carrots does she have after 3 days?

A quick way of writing this is 3(12 − 4) ⟻ The ( ) mean you <u>multiply</u>
what's <u>inside</u> by what's <u>outside</u>.

3×12 3×4

This means 3 × 12 − 3 × 4

So Jane has 36 − 12 = <u>24 carrots</u> after 3 days.

 Greater Depth Jax's pet dinosaur was 220 cm tall when he bought it. It grows at a rate of 120 cm a day. It's now 1180 cm tall. Suggest two different methods you could use to calculate how many days Jax has had the dinosaur for.

"I can solve problems involving addition,
subtraction, multiplication and division."

Practice Questions

1) What is 1359 + 8472?

2) Jenny calculates that 49.73 + 92.12 = 141.85.

   Use rounding to estimate the answer to 49.73 + 92.12
   and say whether you think Jenny's answer is right.

3) List the first six multiples of 5.

4) Is 23 a prime number?

5) Work out the missing numbers in the sum below.

$$
\begin{array}{r}
\square\,3\,8\,1 \\
+\ 1\,5\,\square\,6 \\
\hline
3\,9\,3\,\square
\end{array}
$$

6) What is 8165 − 5329?

7) Write down all the factor pairs of 48.

8) List the common factors of 12, 18 and 40.

9) Tim writes this sequence of square numbers. What is the next number?

   25   36   49   64 $\square$

10) Write down the number that is:

    a) 1000 times bigger than 4.35

    b) one hundred times smaller than 26

Practice Questions

11) Work out in your head:

    a)   11 228 + 2400   b)   8820 − 2100

12) Frog legs cost 9p for a bag of 6.

    a)   Micky has 75p. How many bags of frog legs can he buy?

    b)   Jeff is using a recipe that needs 16 frog legs.
            How many bags does he have to buy?

13) Work out in your head:

    a)   300 ÷ 12   b)   103 × 7

14) Meryl says "I have 5^2 marbles". David says "I have 3^3 marbles".

    a)   How many marbles does Meryl have?

    b)   How many more marbles does David have than Meryl?

15) Ailsa buys six packs of bacon for £3 each.
      Harry spends the same amount of money on nine sausages.

    What is the price of one sausage?

16) Rachel uses 1134 g of cheese to make 9 identical pies.

    How much cheese is in one pie?

17) Sam is making 17 netball skirts for the school team.
      Each skirt needs 1422 mm of fabric.

    a)   Sam estimates how much fabric he'll need by doing 20 × 1500.
            Will his estimate be higher or lower than the actual amount?

    b)   How much fabric does Sam need in total?

18) Kate works in a box factory. She can make 15 boxes in one minute.

    a)   How many minutes will it take her to make 60 boxes?

    b)   How many boxes can she make in one hour? Work it out in your head.

Thousandths

Decimals — the Basics

Decimals are one way to write numbers that <u>aren't whole numbers</u>.

<u>Whole numbers</u> have Ones, Tens, Hundreds and so on.

<u>Decimal numbers</u> also have <u>tenths</u>, <u>hundredths</u> and <u>thousandths</u>...

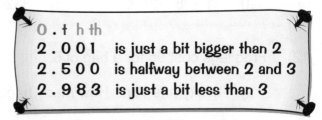

```
O . t h th
2 . 0 0 1    is just a bit bigger than 2
2 . 5 0 0    is halfway between 2 and 3
2 . 9 8 3    is just a bit less than 3
```

Remember, you can partition decimals.
For example 2.983 = 2 + 0.9 + 0.08 + 0.003

You can see where decimals are on a <u>number line</u>.

Each big division shows 1 tenth (0.1) and each small division shows 1 hundredth (0.01):

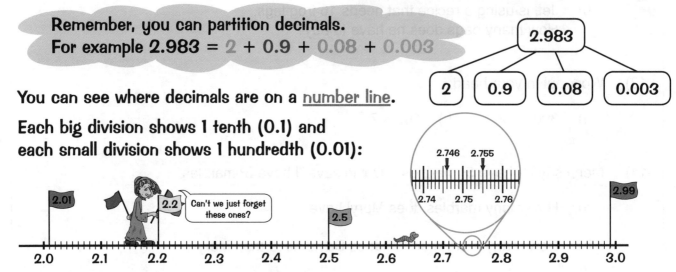

0.001 is One Thousandth

You can write decimals as fractions, and fractions as decimals:

$$\text{One thousandth} = 0.001 = \frac{1}{1000}$$

So... $0.002 = \dfrac{2}{1000}$ (two thousandths) $0.003 = \dfrac{3}{1000}$ (three thousandths) $0.004 = \dfrac{4}{1000}$ (four thousandths) etc...

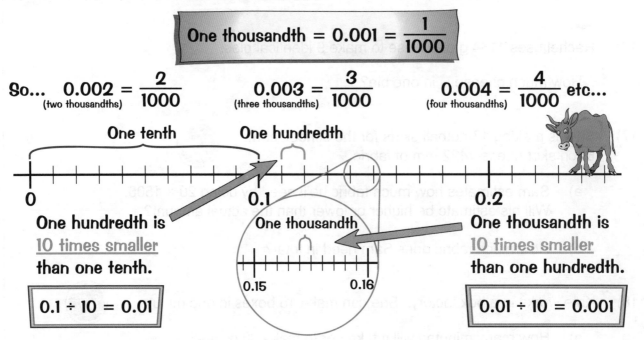

One hundredth is <u>10 times smaller</u> than one tenth.

$$0.1 \div 10 = 0.01$$

One thousandth is <u>10 times smaller</u> than one hundredth.

$$0.01 \div 10 = 0.001$$

"I can write thousandths as fractions or decimals."

Equivalent Fractions

Equivalent Fractions Show the Same Number

Equivalent fractions look different from each other, but they are really the same.

Imagine you and I both have a chocolate bar (the same size).

You split yours into 4 equal pieces and eat 2 of them. ⟹ $\frac{2}{4}$

I split mine into 2 equal pieces and eat 1 of them. ⟹ $\frac{1}{2}$

But from the shading, you can tell we've both eaten the same amount of the chocolate. So $\frac{2}{4}$ and $\frac{1}{2}$ are equivalent fractions.

You can calculate equivalent fractions too. You multiply or divide the numerator and denominator of a fraction by the same number.

Remember:

numerator = top number
denominator = bottom number

EXAMPLES:

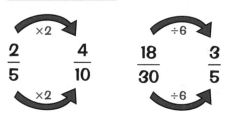

$\frac{2}{5}$ ×2 $\frac{4}{10}$ $\frac{18}{30}$ ÷6 $\frac{3}{5}$

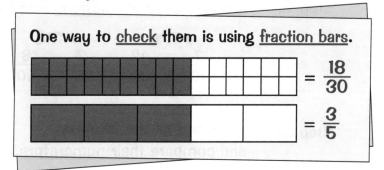

One way to check them is using fraction bars.

$= \frac{18}{30}$

$= \frac{3}{5}$

One Tenth is 10 Hundredths

To convert tenths to hundredths, just multiply the top and bottom of the fraction by 10.
To convert hundredths to tenths, you have to divide the top and bottom by 10.

EXAMPLE:

Write $\frac{3}{10}$ in hundredths.

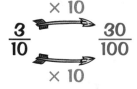

$\frac{3}{10}$ $\xrightarrow{\times 10}$ $\frac{30}{100}$

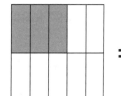 =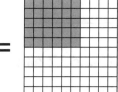

Greater Depth

Fill in the boxes using the numbers below to make 3 equivalent fractions.

3   5   15   25

$\frac{1}{\Box} = \frac{\Box}{\Box} = \frac{5}{\Box}$

"I can recognise and write fractions
that are equivalent to each other."

Ordering Fractions

Putting Fractions in Size Order

If the denominators are the same... ... just compare the **numerators**.
The **bigger** the **numerator**, the **bigger** the fraction.

If the denominators are DIFFERENT... ... **make them the same** by finding **equivalent fractions** (**then** compare the numerators).

EXAMPLE: Order these fractions from smallest to largest: $\frac{7}{10}$, $\frac{2}{15}$ and $\frac{8}{20}$.

Step 1: Decide on a **common denominator**.
60 is a common multiple of 10, 15 and 20, so use 60.

Step 2: Make **equivalent fractions** that have your common denominator.

$$\frac{7}{10} \xrightarrow{\times 6} \frac{42}{60} \qquad \frac{2}{15} \xrightarrow{\times 4} \frac{8}{60} \qquad \frac{8}{20} \xrightarrow{\times 3} \frac{24}{60}$$

Step 3: Write out all the fractions and **compare their numerators**.

$$\frac{42}{60}, \frac{8}{60}, \frac{24}{60}$$ 3 is larger than 2. 2 is larger than 1.

So from smallest to largest, the order is $\frac{8}{60}, \frac{24}{60}, \frac{42}{60}$

Now change the fractions back to the ones in the question.

$$\frac{2}{15}, \frac{8}{20}, \frac{7}{10}$$

EXAMPLE: Order these fractions from smallest to largest: $\frac{1}{3}$, $\frac{5}{6}$ and $\frac{3}{12}$.

3, 6 and 12 all have 12 as a multiple, so use that as the **common denominator**.

Make **equivalent fractions**: $\frac{1}{3} \xrightarrow{\times 4} \frac{4}{12} \qquad \frac{5}{6} \xrightarrow{\times 2} \frac{10}{12}$ ($\frac{3}{12}$ already has 12 as its denominator.)

From smallest to largest, the order is $\frac{3}{12}, \frac{4}{12}, \frac{10}{12}$. ➡ So that's $\frac{3}{12}, \frac{1}{3}, \frac{5}{6}$

"I can compare fractions and order them by their size."

Adding and Subtracting Fractions

Improper Fractions and Mixed Numbers

An **IMPROPER** fraction is one where the numerator is bigger than the denominator. Fractions with a smaller numerator than denominator are called **PROPER FRACTIONS**.

You can change improper fractions into mixed numbers.
MIXED NUMBERS have a whole number bit and a fraction bit.

 IMPROPER FRACTION $\frac{11}{9}$ ...is the same as... $1\frac{2}{9}$  MIXED NUMBER

We've got 11 ninths.
And 9 ninths make up a whole.

So that means we've got one whole and 2 ninths left over.

Using Improper Fractions and Mixed Numbers

You can use improper fractions and mixed numbers to write fractions bigger than 1.

EXAMPLE: Jaival buys some cakes for a party. He cuts each cake into 8 equal slices. At the end of the party he has 13 slices left. Write the number of cakes left as a mixed number.

1 cake = 8 slices. So the number of cakes left as a fraction will have a denominator of 8.

There are 13 slices left. So the number of cakes left is $\frac{13}{8}$.

As a mixed number, the number of cakes left is $\frac{13}{8} = \frac{8}{8} + \frac{5}{8} = 1\frac{5}{8}$

Fractions with the Same Denominator

When fractions have the same denominator, you can add or subtract their numerators.

EXAMPLE: What is $\frac{3}{7} + \frac{10}{7}$?

Add the two numerators together.
The denominator stays the same.

$\frac{3}{7} + \frac{10}{7} = \frac{3+10}{7} = \frac{13}{7}$

To subtract fractions with the same denominator, just subtract the numerators.

$\frac{13}{7}$ is the same as $1\frac{6}{7}$.

 "I can swap between mixed numbers and improper fractions. I can add and subtract fractions with the same denominator."

Adding and Subtracting Fractions

Make Sure the Denominators are the Same

You can _only_ add or subtract fractions with the _same denominator_.

If the denominators are not the same, you have to find a _common denominator_ for your fractions first.

Then you add or subtract the _numerators only_, like before.

EXAMPLE: What is $\frac{1}{2} + \frac{1}{3} - \frac{1}{4}$?

First find _equivalent fractions_ with the same denominator for each.

2, 3 and 4 are all factors of 12, so use 12 as a common denominator.

$$\frac{1}{2} \overset{\times 6}{=} \frac{6}{12} \qquad \frac{1}{3} \overset{\times 4}{=} \frac{4}{12} \qquad \frac{1}{4} \overset{\times 3}{=} \frac{3}{12}$$

Now add and subtract the _numerators_ to get the answer:

$$\frac{1}{2} + \frac{1}{3} - \frac{1}{4} = \frac{6}{12} + \frac{4}{12} - \frac{3}{12} = \frac{6+4-3}{12} = \frac{7}{12}$$

Change Mixed Numbers to Improper Fractions

EXAMPLE:

The film 'Space Cow Returns' is $1\frac{1}{3}$ hours long. Joel watches it for two fifths of an hour. How many hours will it take to watch the rest?

You want to find out $1\frac{1}{3} - \frac{2}{5}$.

The easiest way to do this calculation is to convert $1\frac{1}{3}$ to an _improper fraction_ first.

$$1\frac{1}{3} = \frac{3}{3} + \frac{1}{3} = \frac{4}{3}$$

$$\frac{4}{3} \overset{\times 5}{=} \frac{20}{15} \qquad \frac{2}{5} \overset{\times 3}{=} \frac{6}{15}$$

Now find _equivalent fractions_. 3 and 5 are factors of 15, so use 15 as the common denominator.

Now that the denominators are the same, you can _subtract_ the numerators.

$$1\frac{1}{3} - \frac{2}{5} = \frac{20}{15} - \frac{6}{15} = \frac{20-6}{15} = \frac{14}{15}$$

"I can add and subtract fractions by finding a common denominator."

Section Three — Fractions, Decimals and Percentages

Multiplying with Fractions

"Of" Means Multiply

When you're talking about fractions, "<u>of</u>" just means "<u>times</u>".

So calculating $\frac{1}{4} \times 10$ is the same as finding $\frac{1}{4}$ of 10.

Times by the Top, Divide by the Bottom

To multiply any number by a fraction, you <u>times</u> by the <u>numerator</u> and <u>divide</u> by the <u>denominator</u>.

EXAMPLE: Calculate $\frac{3}{5} \times 15$:

$\frac{3}{5}$ ← Multiply by the numerator.

← Divide by the denominator.

It doesn't matter what order you do it in — just do what's easier.

$15 \div 5 = 3$

$3 \times 3 = 9$

So $\frac{3}{5} \times 15 = \underline{9}$.

EXAMPLE: What is $3\frac{3}{4} \times 12$?

1) <u>Partition</u> $3\frac{3}{4}$ into a <u>whole number</u> and a <u>fraction</u>:

$$3\frac{3}{4} = 3 + \frac{3}{4}$$

2) <u>Multiply</u> the whole number and the fraction by 12 now.

$\frac{3}{4} \times 12$

<u>Multiply</u> 12 by <u>3</u> ━ $12 \times 3 = 36$

<u>Divide</u> by <u>4</u> ━ $36 \div 4 = \underline{9}$

$3 \times 12 = \underline{36}$

3) <u>Add</u> the two answers together. $36 + 9 = 45$

Greater Depth Gaia is trying to work out $\frac{6}{12} \times 4$. She does 4×12 and then divides her answer by 6, to get 8. Explain what Gaia has done wrong and calculate the correct answer.

"I can multiply proper fractions and mixed numbers by whole numbers."

Writing Decimals as Fractions

You Can Turn Decimals into Fractions

To convert a decimal to a fraction, you need to look at the <u>tenths</u>, <u>hundredths</u> and <u>thousandths</u>.

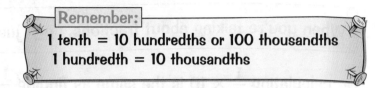

Remember:
1 tenth = 10 hundredths or 100 thousandths
1 hundredth = 10 thousandths

0.3 This decimal is <u>3 tenths</u> so it's equivalent to $\frac{3}{10}$.

0.27 This decimal is 2 tenths and 7 hundredths, which is the same as <u>27 hundredths</u>.

So it's equivalent to $\frac{27}{100}$.

0.521 This decimal is 5 tenths, 2 hundredths and 1 thousandth. That's the same as <u>521 thousandths</u>.

So it's equivalent to $\frac{521}{1000}$.

EXAMPLE: Which fraction is the same as 0.06? Circle your answer.

$\frac{6}{10}$ $\frac{6}{1000}$ $\boxed{\frac{6}{100}}$

The 6 is in the hundredths place so the decimal represents six hundredths.

EXAMPLE: Write 0.71 as a fraction.

0.71 is 7 tenths and 1 hundredth or <u>71 hundredths</u>, so you write it as $\frac{71}{100}$.

EXAMPLE: Write 5.352 as a fraction.

0.352 is 3 tenths and 5 hundredths and 2 thousandths, or <u>352 thousandths</u>.

So 5.352 is <u>5 ones and 352 thousandths</u>.

You can write it as a mixed number. $5\frac{352}{1000}$

"I can read and write decimals as fractions."

Section Three — Fractions, Decimals and Percentages

Rounding Decimals

Rounding Decimals

Rounding decimals is <u>exactly the same</u> as rounding whole numbers.

EXAMPLE:

13   14

A superhero should eat 13.25 kg of baked beans every day. What is 13.25 to the nearest whole number?

13.**2**5 is between 13 and 14.
The decider is 2 so <u>round down</u> to <u>13</u>.

Remember the Rounding Rules

1. The number lies <u>between two possible answers</u>. You have to decide which one it's <u>nearer to</u>.

2. Look at the digit <u>to the right</u> of the place you're rounding to — the DECIDER

3. If the decider is <u>5 or more</u> then <u>round UP</u>. If the decider is <u>less than 5</u> then <u>round DOWN</u>.

Decimal Places Come After the Decimal Point

o . t h th
0.283

1st decimal place
2nd decimal place
3rd decimal place

Each number after the decimal point is called a <u>decimal place</u> (d.p.). They're numbered starting from <u>1</u>.

So if a number has 1 decimal place, it has 1 number after the decimal point.

Rounding to 1 Decimal Place

This is easy if you stick to the <u>rounding rules</u>. You're rounding to 1 d.p. so look at the digit to the right of that — the <u>2nd decimal place</u>, to decide whether to round up or down.

EXAMPLE:

"Super-hamster" has a cape that's 8.35 cm long. What is the length of the cape to 1 decimal place?

8.3   8.4

8.3**5** is between 8.3 and 8.4. The decider is 5 so <u>round up</u> to <u>8.4 cm</u>.

Greater Depth

1) Which of these numbers doesn't round to 4?   3.49   3.75   4.28   3.91

2) How many numbers with 2 decimal places can you think of that round to 1.6?

"I can round decimals with two decimal places to the nearest whole number or to one decimal place."

Ordering and Comparing Decimals

Ordering Decimals

STEP 1) Arrange all the numbers in <u>place value columns</u>.
(Make sure all the decimal points are <u>underneath</u> each other.)

STEP 2) Make them all the <u>same length</u> by filling in extra zeros.

STEP 3) Look at the <u>whole number</u> part of each decimal number.
Arrange the numbers from smallest to largest.

STEP 4) If any whole numbers are the same, look at the digits in the
<u>tenths</u> column. Arrange them from smallest to largest.

STEP 5) If any of the tenths are the same, look at the digits in the
<u>hundredths</u> column. Arrange them from smallest to largest.

STEP 6) If any of the hundredths are the same, look at the digits in the
<u>thousandths</u> column. Arrange them from smallest to largest.

EXAMPLE: Order these numbers from smallest to largest: 0.7, 1.02, 0.295, 0.237, 0.291

STEP 1:	STEP 2:	STEP 3:	STEP 4:	STEP 5:	STEP 6:
0.7	0.700	0.700	0.295	0.237	0.237
1.02	1.020	0.295	0.237	0.295	0.291
0.295	0.295	0.237	0.291	0.291	0.295
0.237	0.237	0.291	0.700	0.700	0.700
0.291	0.291	1.020	1.020	1.020	1.020

So the order is: 0.237, 0.291, 0.295, 0.7, 1.02

Working with Decimals

When adding and subtracting decimals, the important thing to remember is to <u>line up</u> <u>the decimal points</u>. Doing this will help you to answer all kinds of decimal question.

EXAMPLE:

Find the missing digits:

1.97☐ – 0.☐2 = ☐.254

First, <u>line up</u> the decimal points:

Fill in any extra <u>zeros</u> that are needed.

```
  1 . 9 7 ☐
– 0 . ☐ 2 0
─────────────
  ☐ . 2 5 4
```

1) ☐ – 0 = 4
The missing number here has to be 4.

2) 9 – ☐ = 2
The missing number here has to be 7.

3) 1 – 0 = ☐
The missing number here is 1.

So the answer is 1.974 – 0.72 = 1.254

"I can read, write, compare and solve problems with numbers with up to 3 decimal places."

Section Three — Fractions, Decimals and Percentages

Percentages

"Per Cent" Means "Out of 100"

% is a short way of writing <u>per cent</u> and it just means "out of 100".

So 20% ("twenty per cent") is <u>20 out of 100</u>. (Or 20 parts in every 100.)

<u>100%</u> is the <u>total</u> amount (here it's the total number of squares).

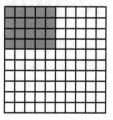

EXAMPLE: 52% of a class own pets. What % of the class don't own pets?

The <u>whole</u> class is <u>100%</u>. 100 − 52 = 48, so <u>48%</u> of the class don't own pets.

You Can Convert Percentages to Fractions

You can write any percentage as a <u>fraction</u>:

$20\% = \dfrac{20}{100}$

Put the <u>percentage</u> on the <u>top</u>...

...and <u>100</u> on the <u>bottom</u> of the fraction.

EXAMPLE: Bhavna and Hank each enter a camel into the same series of races.

Bhavna's camel wins 16% of the races. Hank's camel wins $\dfrac{3}{10}$ of the races. Whose camel wins the most races?

Convert the percentage to a <u>fraction</u>.

16 goes on top.   100 goes on the bottom.

$16\% = \dfrac{16}{100}$

Both fractions need to have the <u>same denominator</u>, so convert $\dfrac{3}{10}$ to <u>hundredths</u>.
Compare the <u>numerators</u>.

$\dfrac{3}{10} = \dfrac{30}{100}$ ×10

30 is bigger than 16, so <u>Hank's camel</u> wins the most races.

Converting Between % and Decimals is Easy

% to Decimals
1) All you do is <u>divide by 100</u>.
2) That just means moving the digits <u>two places to the right</u>.

Decimals to %
1) This is just the <u>opposite</u>, so you <u>multiply by 100</u>.
2) All you have to do is move the digits <u>two places to the left</u>.

EXAMPLES:
a) Convert 26% to a decimal. → **a) 26% = 26 ÷ 100 = 0.26**
b) Convert 0.85 to a percentage. → **b) 0.85 × 100% = 85%**

"I know what % means and I can write percentages as fractions or decimals."

Percentages, Fractions and Decimals

Learn these Percentages, Decimals and Fractions

You can write <u>any</u> fraction as a <u>percentage</u> as well as a <u>decimal</u>.

Here are some common ones you should know.

0    $\frac{1}{4}$ $\frac{1}{2}$ $\frac{3}{4}$ 1

0.25 or 25%   0.5 or 50%   0.75 or 75%

0    $\frac{1}{5}$ $\frac{2}{5}$ $\frac{4}{5}$ 1

0.2 or 20%   0.4 or 40%   0.8 or 80%

0   $\frac{1}{10}$ 1

0.1 or 10%

Converting other fractions into percentages and decimals is easy... if you know how...

You can Convert Fractions to Percentages...

To convert a fraction to a percentage, you need to make an <u>equivalent fraction</u> with <u>100 as the denominator</u>.

EXAMPLES:

× 10
$$\frac{6}{10} = \frac{60}{100} = 60\%$$
× 10

× 4
$$\frac{2}{25} = \frac{8}{100} = 8\%$$
× 4

× 2
$$\frac{17}{50} = \frac{34}{100} = 34\%$$
× 2

÷ 2
$$\frac{14}{200} = \frac{7}{100} = 7\%$$
÷ 2

...and also to Decimals

To convert a fraction to a decimal, make an equivalent fraction over 10, 100 or 1000. Then read off the number of <u>tenths</u>, <u>hundredths</u> or <u>thousandths</u>.

EXAMPLE: Write $2\frac{1}{10}$ as a decimal.

This fraction already has 10 as the denominator so you don't need to change it.

First, change the fraction part to a <u>decimal</u>. $\frac{1}{10}$ is <u>1 tenth</u>, so it's equivalent to 0.1.

Next, add the <u>whole number</u> bit back on to the decimal.   2 + 0.1 = 2.1

Greater Depth

1) What are four different fractions that are equal to 0.4?

2) Find one decimal that is bigger and one decimal that is smaller than $\frac{13}{20}$.

"I can convert fractions into percentages and decimals."

Section Three — Fractions, Decimals and Percentages

Fraction, Decimal and Percentage Problems

Find a Percentage of an Amount

EXAMPLE: Jack is saving up to buy a new bike that costs £500. So far he has saved 78% of the cost. How much money has he saved?

First change the percentage to a <u>fraction</u>.

$$78\% = \frac{78}{100}$$

So you want to calculate $\frac{78}{100}$ of £500.

First divide by the denominator...

£500 ÷ 100 = 5

...then multiply by the numerator.

5 × 78 = 390

So Jack has saved £390 so far.

EXAMPLE: Molly owns a herd of sheep that are either blue or purple. $\frac{1}{5}$ of the herd is blue. What percentage of the herd is purple?

$\frac{1}{5}$ is the same as 20%. The whole herd is 100%.

So the percentage of sheep that are purple is: 100% − 20% = 80%

So <u>80%</u> of the herd is purple.

Write an Amount as a Percentage of Another

EXAMPLE: Gerald needs 1000 frogs to make frog soup. He collects 550. What percentage of his total is this?

1) Write 550 out of 1000 as a fraction: $\frac{550}{1000}$

2) Make an equivalent fraction with <u>100</u> as the denominator.

3) Now the numerator is the percentage.

$$\frac{550}{1000} = \frac{55}{100} = 55\%$$
(÷ 10)

<u>Another Method:</u>

Convert the fraction into a decimal...

$\frac{550}{1000} = 0.55$

...then the decimal into a percentage.

0.55 × 100% = 55%

"I can solve problems that involve fractions, decimals and percentages."

Practice Questions

1) Write thirteen thousandths as a fraction.

2) Write these decimals as fractions:

   a) 0.27   b) 0.91   c) 0.03

3) Round 7.68 to the nearest whole number.

4) Write these decimals in order from smallest to largest:

   0.223   0.05   1.01   0.056   0.227

5) What is $\frac{7}{4}$ as a mixed number?

6) Round 0.36 to 1 decimal place.

7) Which one of these fractions is equivalent to $\frac{3}{5}$?

   $\frac{12}{15}$ $\frac{6}{10}$ $\frac{5}{3}$ $\frac{9}{10}$

8) Order these fractions from smallest to largest:

   $\frac{12}{16}$ $\frac{2}{8}$ $\frac{2}{4}$

9) In the Frog-Olympics, Freddie the frog won 28% of his races.
   Frances the frog won $\frac{6}{25}$ of her races.

   Who won the larger percentage of races?

Section Three — Fractions, Decimals and Percentages

Practice Questions

10) Write the answers to these calculations as mixed numbers.

 a) $\dfrac{2}{5} + \dfrac{9}{10}$ b) $\dfrac{5}{7} \times 12$ c) $2\dfrac{5}{12} - \dfrac{5}{6}$

11) Edith is throwing a party and invites 18 guests. Every guest gets $\dfrac{2}{3}$ of a cake each.

 How many cakes does she need to make?

12) Lisa has £53. She spends £26.99 on a rocking chair.

 How much money does she have left?

13) Write these numbers as percentages.

 a) $\dfrac{12}{25}$ b) $\dfrac{7}{10}$ c) 0.51

14) Marilyn has a herd of 50 llamas. Bert buys 14 llamas from Marilyn.

 What percentage of the herd does Bert buy?

15) James has 200 sweets. He gives 15% of them to his friend.

 How many sweets does James have left?

16) Sally and Hassan share a chocolate bar.
 Sally eats $\dfrac{1}{4}$ of the chocolate bar and Hassan eats $\dfrac{2}{5}$.

 a) How much more chocolate has Hassan eaten than Sally?

 b) The bar has a mass of 100 g. How much is left?

Metric Units

Sometimes You Need to Convert Units

You can change from one unit into another.

1 km = 1000 m
1 m = 100 cm
1 cm = 10 mm

1 kg = 1000 g
1 l = 1000 ml

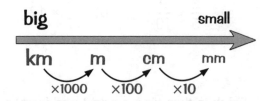

big   small

km   m   cm   mm

×1000   ×100   ×10

EXAMPLE:

Bucket A has a capacity of 6.2 l. Bucket B has a capacity of 6300 ml.
Which bucket can hold more wormy sludge?

Put both capacities into the same units.

So to convert l to ml, multiply by 1000.

Bucket A's capacity = 6.2 × 1000 = 6200 ml

6300 ml is more than 6200 ml.
So Bucket B can hold more wormy sludge.

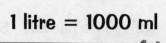

1 litre = 1000 ml

EXAMPLE:

Mohit can jump 1.8 m. Kyle can jump 20 centimetres further.
How far can Kyle jump in centimetres?

You need to give your answer in centimetres,
so convert all the units into centimetres.

1 m = 100 cm

So 1.8 m = 1.8 × 100 cm = 180 cm.
So Kyle can jump 180 cm + 20 cm = 200 cm.

EXAMPLE:

An old robot has a mass of 3400 g. A new robot weighs
400 grams less. What is the mass of the new robot in kilograms?

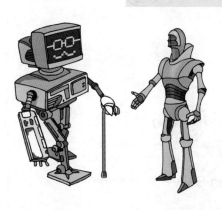

The new robot's mass is 3400 g – 400 g = 3000 g.
But you need to give your answer in kilograms...

1 kg = 1000 g

So to convert grams to kg, divide by 1000.
So 3000 g ÷ 1000 = 3 kg.

"I can convert between different units."

Imperial Units

Units Can be Metric or Imperial

Metric units are used more commonly now than imperial units.

Some metric units...
grams metres kilograms
millilitres litres centimetres

Some imperial units...
miles inches ounces pints
feet pounds yards

You Can Convert Between Metric and Imperial

You can convert imperial units to metric units, or the other way round.
For example, you could change a distance in feet to a distance in metres.

Make sure you know these common conversions:

1 metre ≈ 3 feet   5 centimetres ≈ 2 inches
1 kilogram ≈ 2 pounds   8 kilometres ≈ 5 miles
1 litre ≈ 2 pints   100 grams ≈ 4 ounces

The sign '≈' means 'is approximately equal to'. These conversions aren't exact but it's fine to use them for rough calculations.

EXAMPLE: Jacinda finds a huge slug that weighs 12 kg. Approximately how heavy is the slug in pounds?

Step 1) Find the conversion fact you need: here it's 1 kg ≈ 2 pounds.

Step 2) Every 1 kilogram is 2 pounds, so you will have twice as many pounds as kilograms. So you need to multiply by 2.

$12 \times 2 = 24$

Step 3) So the slug weighs approximately 24 pounds.

EXAMPLE: Approximately how far is 40 miles in kilometres?

Find the conversion fact you need: here it's 5 miles ≈ 8 kilometres.

40 miles is 8 lots of 5 miles.
That's equal to about 8 lots of 8 km.

8×8 km = 64 km

 Four tennis balls weigh 8 ounces in total.
Describe how you could work out approximately how much this is in kilograms.

"I can convert roughly between imperial and metric units."

Perimeter

Finding the Perimeters of Shapes

1) To find a <u>perimeter</u>, just <u>add up</u> the lengths of all the sides.
2) Make sure you get <u>all</u> the sides.
   It's best to <u>mark</u> one vertex with a blob or cross...
3) ...then work your way around the shape, <u>adding</u> as you go.

EXAMPLE:

This is Katie the Giant's desk. What is its perimeter?

You've been given the lengths of all the sides apart from <u>this one</u>...

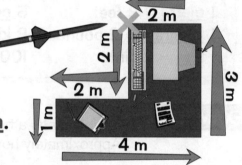

The 'missing' side plus 2 m (by the computer keyboard) must be the same length as the side opposite, which is 3 m. So the missing side must be 3 m – 2 m = <u>1 m</u>.

Put a <u>big cross</u> on one vertex, then work around the shape.

The perimeter is:

$2 + 2 + 1 + 4 + 3 + 2 = \underline{14 \text{ m}}$.

You Might Have to Measure some Sides

You won't always be told the measurements.

EXAMPLE:

This shape is made from three regular hexagons. Find its perimeter.

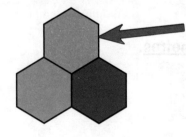

No lengths are marked on so <u>measure</u> the sides. Luckily you don't have to measure <u>all</u> of them... They're <u>regular</u> hexagons so <u>all</u> the sides are the <u>same length</u>.

<u>One side</u> is <u>9 mm</u> long.
The perimeter is made up of <u>four sides</u> from <u>each hexagon</u>.
There are <u>three</u> hexagons, so $4 \times 3 = \underline{12}$ sides altogether.

So the perimeter = $12 \times 9 \text{ mm} = \underline{108 \text{ mm}}$.

"I can measure and calculate the perimeters of shapes." ✓ ✓ ✓

Perimeter

There Can Be More Than One Missing Length

EXAMPLE: Find the perimeter of this block of cheese.

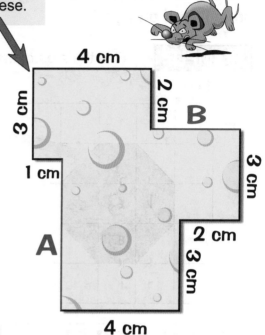

Before you can find the perimeter you need to work out some missing lengths — sides A and B.

Add up the vertical lengths down the right-hand side to find the height of the cheese.
So 2 cm + 3 cm + 3 cm = 8 cm
So A must be 8 cm – 3 cm = 5 cm

Do the same thing with the horizontal measurements to find the width of the cheese.
So 1 cm + 4 cm + 2 cm = 7 cm
So B must be 7 cm – 4 cm = 3 cm

Add up the sides:
4 + 2 + 3 + 3 + 2 + 3 + 4 + 5 + 1 + 3 = 30 cm

EXAMPLE: This snazzy rectangle has a perimeter of 22 cm and a width of 4 cm. Find the length of side x.

As it's a rectangle the top and bottom must both be 4 cm. The left and right sides must both measure x cm.

So to get the perimeter you would do:
4 + x + 4 + x = 22   which is the same as   8 + 2x = 22

You need to get x on its own.
$8 + 2x = 22$
So... $2x = 22 - 8$
$2x = 14$
Then divide by 2 to get x on its own
$x = 14 \div 2$
$x = 7$

So the length of side x is 7 cm.

Whatever is done on one side of the "=" must be done on the other side as well.

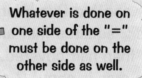

x

4 cm

"I can measure and calculate the perimeters of shapes."

Area

You Can Estimate Area by Counting Squares...

You can find areas by counting <u>how many squares</u> or <u>half-squares</u> are covered on a grid.

EXAMPLE: Find the area of the shape below.

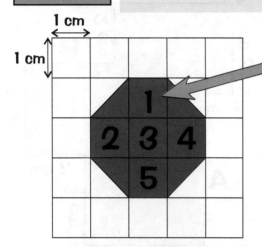

1) Count the number of <u>whole squares</u>. There are 5 whole squares = 5 cm².

2) The shape also covers <u>4 half squares</u>. So the area covered by the half squares is

$$\frac{1}{2} \text{ cm} + \frac{1}{2} \text{ cm} + \frac{1}{2} \text{ cm} + \frac{1}{2} \text{ cm} = 2 \text{ cm}$$

3) So the total area of the shape is

$$5 \text{ cm}^2 + 2 \text{ cm}^2 = \underline{7 \text{ cm}^2}$$

...But Not All Shapes Fit Neatly

Not all shapes fit neatly into whole or half squares. You can <u>estimate</u> the areas of these shapes by counting <u>how many squares</u> are <u>more than half covered</u>.

EXAMPLE: <u>4</u> squares are more than half covered by this boring purple blob. So its area is about <u>4 cm²</u>.

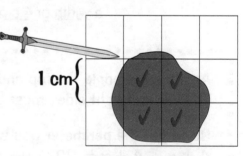

ANOTHER EXAMPLE:

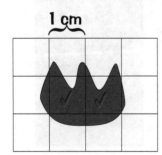

This footprint was left by a lesser spotted Cumbrian Yeti. It has <u>2</u> squares that are <u>more</u> than half covered. So its area is about <u>2 cm²</u>.

Look at the shape on the square grid on the right. Keziah says the shape has an area of 8 cm². Suggest two things that Keziah has done wrong when estimating the area of the shape.

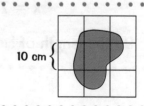

"I can estimate the area of irregular shapes."

Area

Area of Squares and Rectangles — Just Multiply

There's a quick way of working out the <u>areas</u> of <u>squares</u> and <u>rectangles</u> to save you the hassle of counting all the squares.

Count how many squares <u>long</u> the shape is.
Then count how many squares <u>wide</u> it is.
Then <u>multiply</u> these numbers together.

I am the Count and I like to count squares. Von, two, three...

EXAMPLE: Work out the area of this square.

There are 4 rows of 4 squares.
So the area is $4 \times 4 = \underline{16}$

16 what? 16 elephants? Nope. Each square has sides 1 cm long, so they're <u>square centimetres</u>.
So the answer is <u>16 square centimetres</u> or $\underline{16 \text{ cm}^2}$.

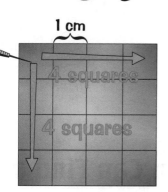

1 cm

4 squares

4 squares

You Might Need to Measure the Sides

If a rectangle or square isn't on a grid, you can just <u>measure</u> its length and width.

Area = length × width

EXAMPLE: Work out the area of a rectangle measuring 9 cm by 7 cm.

Just multiply the sides together. Area = $9 \times 7 = \underline{63 \text{ cm}^2}$

Sometimes There's a Length Missing

EXAMPLE: A rectangle has a width of <u>5 cm</u> and an area of <u>35 cm²</u>. What is its length?

Area = length × width, so, 35 = length × 5

    5 multiplies by 7 to give 35...

        ...so the rectangle has a length of <u>7 cm</u>.

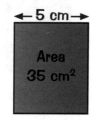

← 5 cm →

Area
35 cm²

"I can calculate the area of squares and rectangles and use units like cm² and m²."

Estimating Volume and Capacity

Volume is Measured in Cubic Units

The <u>volume</u> of a shape is the <u>amount of space</u> it takes up.

Volume is measured in <u>cubic units</u>, like <u>cubic centimetres</u> (cm³) or <u>cubic metres</u> (m³).

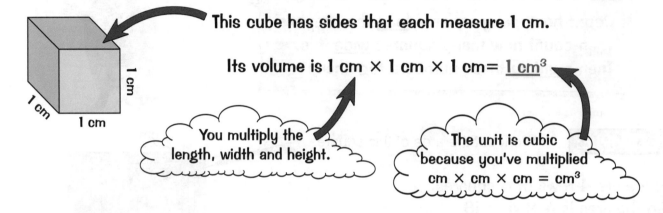

This cube has sides that each measure 1 cm.

Its volume is 1 cm × 1 cm × 1 cm= <u>1 cm³</u>

You multiply the length, width and height.

The unit is cubic because you've multiplied cm × cm × cm = cm³

You Can Find a Volume by Counting Cubes

Imagine that a <u>cuboid</u> is made up of <u>cubes</u> with sides of <u>1 cm</u>. The <u>volume</u> of the cuboid is the same as the <u>number of cubes</u>:

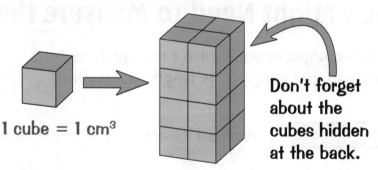

1 cube = 1 cm³

Don't forget about the cubes hidden at the back.

16 cubes = 16 cm³

EXAMPLE: Find the volume of the cuboid.

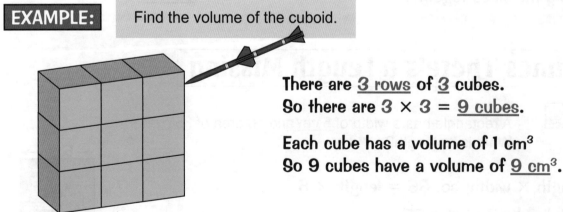

1 cube = 1 cm³

There are <u>3 rows</u> of <u>3</u> cubes.
So there are 3 × 3 = <u>9 cubes</u>.

Each cube has a volume of 1 cm³
So 9 cubes have a volume of <u>9 cm³</u>.

"I can estimate volume and capacity."

Estimating Volume and Capacity

You Can Count Cubes for All Sorts of Shapes

EXAMPLE: Find the volume of this 3D shape.

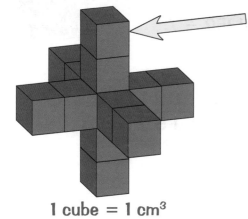

1 cube = 1 cm³

There are 6 sticky-outy bits.
Each contains 2 cubes.
That's 6 × 2 = 12 cubes.

There's also going to be a cube in the centre.
So do 12 + 1 = 13 cubes in total.

Each cube has a volume of 1 cm³.
So 13 cubes have a volume of <u>13 cm³</u>.

EXAMPLE: Find the volume of this 3D S shape.

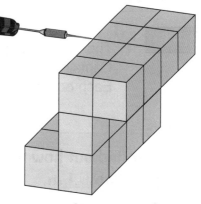

1 cube = 1 cm³

The S shape is made up of <u>5 cubes</u>.
It's 4 cubes deep, so do 5 × 4 = <u>20 cubes</u>.

Each cube has a volume of 1 cm³.
So 20 cubes have a volume of <u>20 cm³</u>.

Capacity is How Much a Container Can Hold

<u>Liquids</u> have a <u>volume</u>. This is the <u>amount of space</u> they take up.
The <u>largest volume</u> of liquid something <u>can hold</u> is called its <u>capacity</u>.

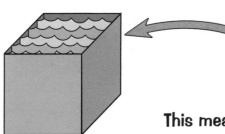

This container has a <u>volume</u> of 9 cm³.
So it also has a <u>capacity</u> of 9 cm³.

This means it could hold <u>9 cm³</u> of water.

"I can estimate volume and capacity."

Solving Time and Measurement Problems

Some Problems Could Involve Converting Time

EXAMPLE: A snail completes the Lancaster Fun Run in <u>152 days</u>. How long is this in <u>weeks and days</u>?

There are 7 days in a week, so you need to work out 152 ÷ 7.

You can work this out by short division.

So 152 ÷ 7 = <u>21 remainder 5</u>
This just means **21 weeks and 5 days.**

$$
\begin{array}{r}
0\ 2\ 1\ _r5 \\
7\overline{)\ 1^15^52}
\end{array}
$$

So the snail took <u>21 weeks and 5 days</u>.

Choose the Easiest Way to Do Things

EXAMPLE: The mast of Captain Sam's ship is <u>5.1 m</u> high. Captain Sam makes a tower of <u>boxes</u> that reaches the top of the mast. Each box is <u>93 cm</u> tall. How many boxes does Captain Sam use?

You have to find out how many times <u>93 cm</u> goes into <u>5.1 m</u>.

Change the 5.1 m into <u>cm</u> first.
5.1 × 100 = <u>510 cm</u>

MAKE SURE THE <u>UNITS</u> MATCH.

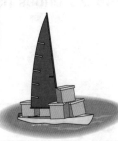

So now the problem is '<u>How many 93s go into 510</u>?'

You can use <u>estimation</u> here too. 93 cm is <u>nearly 100 cm</u>.
If the boxes were 100 cm tall, 5 boxes would reach 500 cm.
So you would need <u>6 boxes</u> to get to 510 cm.
Check that 6 × 93 cm would be tall enough.

$$
\begin{array}{r}
9\ 3 \\
\times\ \ \ 6 \\
\hline
5\ 5\ 8 \\
{\scriptstyle 1}
\end{array}
$$

So <u>93 × 6 = 558 cm</u>

558 cm is high enough.
So Captain Sam uses <u>6 boxes</u>.

"I can solve problems that involve converting between units."

Solving Time and Measurement Problems

Some Problems use Percentages and Fractions

EXAMPLE: Erica drinks 25% of a 500 ml bottle of cola. How many millilitres is this?

You can work this out really quickly if you remember that 25% = $\frac{1}{4}$.

So you just need to divide 500 ml by 4.
OR halve it twice if you find that easier.

$$500 \text{ ml} \div 4 = 125 \text{ ml}$$

Break Problems Down into Simple Steps

EXAMPLE: Maya earns £6 an hour. She works for 12 hours. John earns three times as much as Maya per hour. John works for 7 hours.

How much more will John earn than Maya?

Work out how much John earns per hour: £6 × 3 = £18

Then find out how much they each earn in total.

Maya gets £6 × 12 = £72.

John earns £18 an hour and works for 7 hours.
So he gets £18 × 7 = £126.

$$\begin{array}{r} 1\,8 \\ \times\ \ 7 \\ \hline 1\,2\,6 \\ 5 \end{array}$$

Now work out the difference.

$$\begin{array}{r} {}^1{1}2\,6 \\ -\ \ 7\,2 \\ \hline 5\,4 \end{array}$$

So John earns £54 more than Maya.

EXAMPLE: A teacher buys 2 bags of sweets. One weighs 2.45 kg and the other weighs 1.72 kg. She splits the sweets evenly between 100 pupils.

What mass of sweets does each pupil get to the nearest gram?

First, add together the weights.
So she has 4.17 kg of sweets.

$$\begin{array}{r} 2.4\,5 \\ +1.7\,2 \\ \hline 4.1\,7 \\ 1 \end{array}$$

Convert 4.17 kg into grams, so 4.17 kg × 1000 = 4170 g.
Now divide between the 100 pupils, so do 4170 g ÷ 100 = 41.7 g.

Round to the nearest gram. So 41.7 rounds up to 42.0

So the pupils get 42 grams each.

"I can solve problems involving money and measurements."

Practice Questions

1) Convert 3.4 kg into grams.

2) Convert 2600 metres into km.

3) Sarah goes on holiday for 15 days.

   How long is this in weeks and days?

4) The diagram on the right shows a plan of a room.

   What is the perimeter of the room?

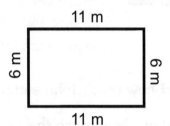

11 m

6 m

6 m

11 m

5) A rectangular rug measures 3 m by 4 m.

   What is its area?

6) Estimate the area of the shape on the grid.

   Each square has an area of 1 cm².

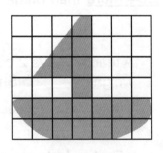

Not to scale

7) What is the volume of the shape on the right?

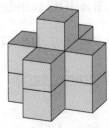

1 cube = 1 cm³

Practice Questions

8) Which measurement is bigger?

    a) 4 kg or 6 pounds?

    b) 16.5 litres or 1650 ml?

    c) 18 litres or 30 pints?

9) Shaun has 2 litres of orange juice. He drinks 4 cups of juice.

    Each cup holds 300 ml of juice. How much juice is left in the carton?
Show your working.

10) The shape on the right has two measurements missing.

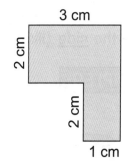

    Find the perimeter of the shape.

11) Arthur's field is a rectangle that measures 20 metres by 15 metres. He wants to put a fence around the outside.

    Arthur has 60 metres of fencing. Will he have enough?
Show your working.

12) Ash's garden measures 4 metres by 5 metres.
Her garden has a pond that measures 2 metres by 3 metres.

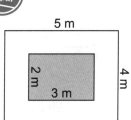

    Calculate the area of Ash's garden that surrounds the pond.
Show your working.

13) A rectangle has a length of 6 cm and a perimeter of 22 cm.

    Calculate its width.

3D Shapes

3D Shapes are Solid Shapes

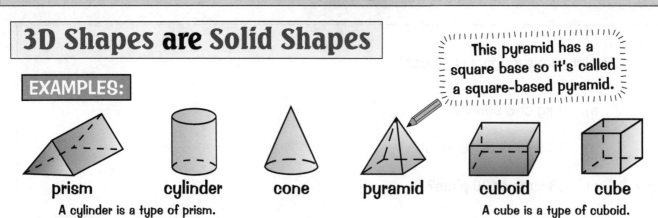

EXAMPLES:

prism   cylinder   cone   pyramid   cuboid   cube

This pyramid has a square base so it's called a square-based pyramid.

A cylinder is a type of prism.
(A prism is a type of 3D shape where the two end faces are exactly the same.)

A cube is a type of cuboid.

Plans/Elevations — 2D Views of 3D Shapes

A <u>PLAN</u> is the view from <u>directly above</u> an object.

An <u>ELEVATION</u> is the view from <u>one side</u> (elevations are also called <u>projections</u>).
Elevations might be <u>different</u> depending on whether you're looking from the
<u>front</u> or the <u>side</u> (like for the triangular prism below).

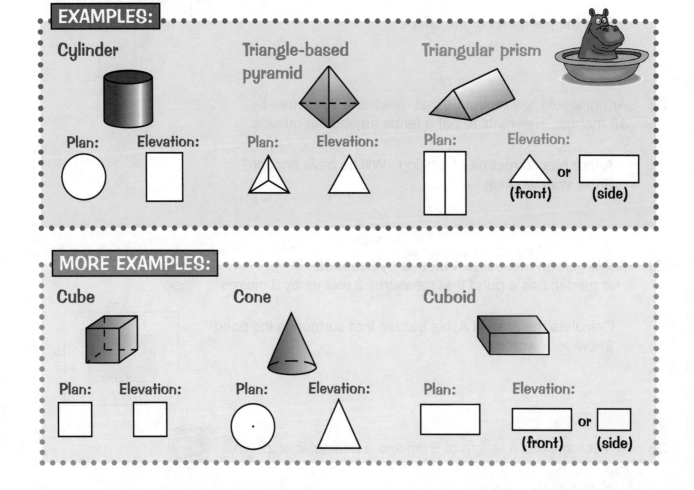

EXAMPLES:

Cylinder

Triangle-based pyramid

Triangular prism

Plan: Elevation: Plan: Elevation: Plan: Elevation:

or
(front)   (side)

MORE EXAMPLES:

Cube

Cone

Cuboid

Plan: Elevation: Plan: Elevation: Plan: Elevation:

or
(front)   (side)

"I can recognise 3D shapes from their plans and elevations."

3D Shapes

A Shape Net Folds Up to Make a 3D Shape

If you take a cardboard box apart you're left with the net.

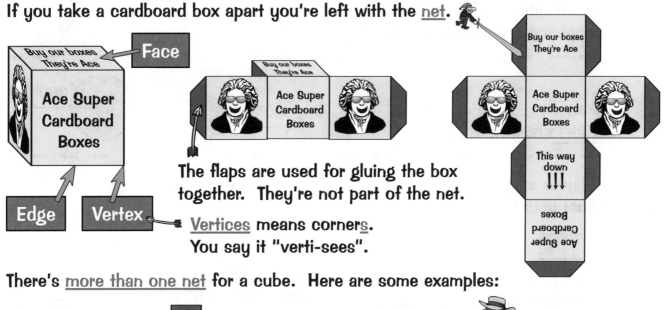

The flaps are used for gluing the box together. They're not part of the net.

Vertices means corners.
You say it "verti-sees".

There's more than one net for a cube. Here are some examples:

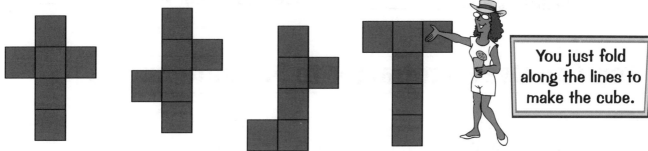

You just fold along the lines to make the cube.

All 3D Shapes Have Nets

All 3D shapes have nets.

Each face of the 3D shape has to match up with one part of the net.

Triangular Prism

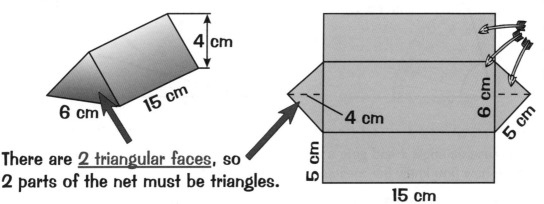

You can't see these three faces in the 3D picture.

There are 2 triangular faces, so 2 parts of the net must be triangles.

"I can recognise a 3D shape from its net."

Angles

You Can Estimate Angles

You can estimate how big an angle
is by comparing it to one of these.

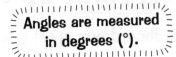

Angles are measured
in degrees (°).

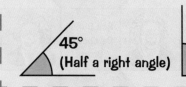 45°
(Half a right angle)

 90°

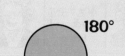 180°

 270°

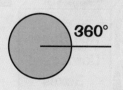 360°

Decide if your angle is a <u>bit smaller</u> or <u>larger</u> than one of these,
then adjust your estimate.

EXAMPLES:

This angle is bit less than 90°.
I'd estimate that it's 80°.

This is about a right
angle and a half. If you
ask me, I'd say it's about
135° (90° + 45° = 135°).

You Can Use a Protractor to Measure Angles

1. Put the <u>cross on the</u>
<u>protractor</u> over the
<u>vertex</u> of the angle.

2. <u>Line up</u> the <u>bottom line</u>
<u>on the protractor</u> with
one line of your angle.

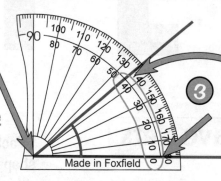

Made in Foxfield

3. Just <u>read</u> the scale. <u>45°</u>
Use the scale that has <u>0</u>
on the line of your angle.

EXAMPLES:

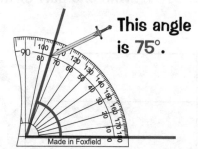
This angle
is 75°.

Made in Foxfield

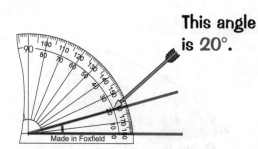
This angle
is 20°.

Made in Foxfield

Greater Depth

1) Emi measures angle x and gets a value of 100°.
Explain how you know her measurement is incorrect.

2) Suggest one mistake Emi might have made when using her protractor.

 x

"I know that angles are measured in degrees. I can
estimate angles, and use a protractor to measure them."

 ✓ ✓ ✓ ✓

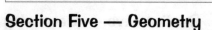

Angles

You Can Use a Protractor to Draw Angles

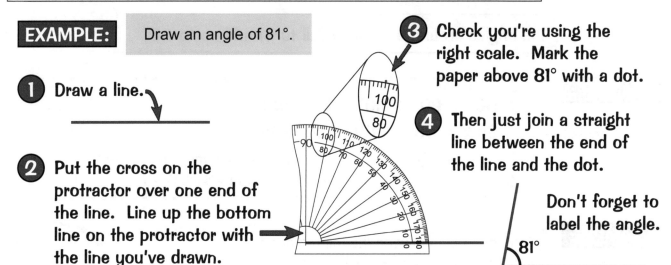

EXAMPLE: Draw an angle of 81°.

1 Draw a line.

2 Put the cross on the protractor over one end of the line. Line up the bottom line on the protractor with the line you've drawn.

3 Check you're using the right scale. Mark the paper above 81° with a dot.

4 Then just join a straight line between the end of the line and the dot.

Don't forget to label the angle.

81°

Different Size Angles have Different Names

Angles are given different <u>names</u> according to how <u>big</u> they are:

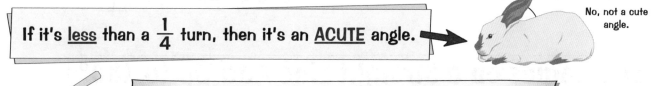

If it's <u>less</u> than a $\frac{1}{4}$ turn, then it's an <u>ACUTE</u> angle.

No, not a cute angle.

If it's <u>exactly</u> a $\frac{1}{4}$ turn, then it's a <u>RIGHT</u> angle.

If it's between a $\frac{1}{4}$ and $\frac{1}{2}$ turn, then it's an <u>OBTUSE</u> angle.

If it's <u>more</u> than a $\frac{1}{2}$ turn, then it's a <u>REFLEX</u> angle.

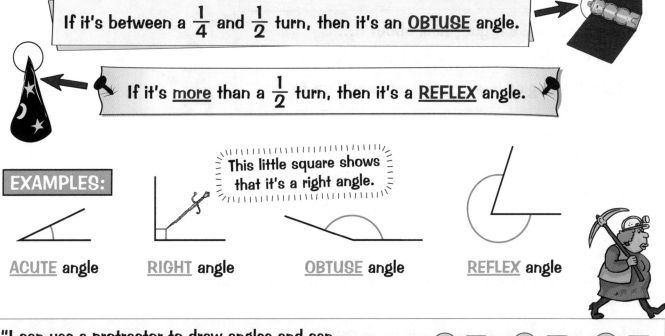

EXAMPLES:

This little square shows that it's a right angle.

<u>ACUTE</u> angle   <u>RIGHT</u> angle   <u>OBTUSE</u> angle   <u>REFLEX</u> angle

---

"I can use a protractor to draw angles and can identify acute, obtuse, reflex and right angles."

Angle Rules

The Angles Around a Point Add Up to 360°

> The angles around a point (a full turn) add up to 360°.

EXAMPLE:

Find angle k.

$90° + 90° + 110° + k = 360°$

So $k = 360° - 110° - 90° - 90°$

$\quad = \underline{70°}$

The squares show that these angles are right angles (90°).

EXAMPLE:

Find the angle between the minute hand and the hour hand of a clock at 5 pm.

There are 360 degrees in the full circle. They are divided into 12 by the numbers on the clock. ➡ $360° \div 12 = 30°$

There are five 30° bits between the minute hand and the hour hand.

So the angle between the hands must be $30° \times 5 = \underline{150°}$

The Angles on a Straight Line Add Up to 180°

> The angles that meet on a straight line (half a turn) add up to 180°.

It makes sense if you think about it...
If the angles in a whole turn add up to 360°,
then the angles in a $\frac{1}{2}$ turn must add up to 180°.

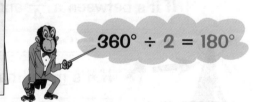

$360° \div 2 = 180°$

EXAMPLE:

Find angle a.

$95° + 60° + a = 180°$

So $a = 180° - 95° - 60° = \underline{25°}$

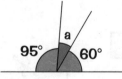

Greater Depth

Three angles meet on a straight line. One of the angles measures 50°.
Suggest a possible pair of values for the other two angles.

"I know that angles at a point add up to 360° and that angles on a straight line add up to 180°."

Angle Rules

Angles at a Quarter Turn Add Up to 90°

The angles that meet at a quarter turn add up to 90°.

If the angles in a whole turn add up to 360°, then the angles in a $\frac{1}{4}$ turn must add up to 90°.

$360° \div 4 = 90°$

EXAMPLE:

Find angle z.

$32° + z = 90°$

So $z = 90° - 32° = \underline{58°}$

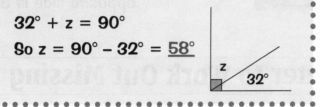

z

32°

Angles at a 3-Quarter Turn Add Up to 270°

The angles that meet at a three-quarter turn add up to 270°.

If the angles in a $\frac{1}{4}$ turn add up to 90° then the angles in a $\frac{3}{4}$ turn must add up to 270°.

$90° \times 3 = 270°$

EXAMPLE: Find angle f.

160° 75°

f

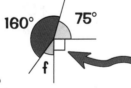

This is a right angle (90°).
You know that angles at a point add up to 360° so you could also find f by doing:
$360° - 160° - 75° - 90° = 35°$

$160° + 75° + f = 270°$

So $f = 270° - 160° - 75° = \underline{35°}$

You can use <u>angle rules</u> to <u>solve problems</u>...

EXAMPLE:

Kate has a list of angles. Will says that <u>these angles could lie on a straight line</u>. How does he know this?

Kate's Angles

24°   46°
51°   59°

The <u>angles</u> in the list add up to <u>180°</u>
$46° + 51° + 24° + 59° = \underline{180°}$

So, Kate's angles could lie on a <u>straight line</u>.

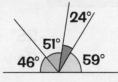

24°
51°
46°   59°

"I know that angles at a quarter turn add up to 90°
and that angles at a three-quarter turn add up to 270°."

Angles and Sides of Rectangles

Rectangles Have Two Pairs of Equal Sides

If you know the length of one side of a rectangle, you know the length of the opposite side.

EXAMPLE: What is the length of side x?

The opposite sides of a rectangle are parallel — they are always the same distance apart and they never meet or cross.

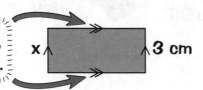

Matching arrows show parallel sides.

x ↑   ↑ 3 cm

x = 3 cm because the opposite side is 3 cm.

Use the Perimeter to Work Out Missing Sides

The perimeter is the total distance around the outside of a shape.
You can use the perimeter of a rectangle to work out the length of missing sides.

EXAMPLE: The perimeter of this pitch is 150 m.
What are the lengths of the missing sides?

b

a   c

50 m

1 You know that b = 50 m because the opposite side is 50 m.

2 The perimeter of the pitch is 150 m so....

50 + 50 + a + c = 150

So a + c = 150 − 50 − 50
a + c = 50

3 You know that a and c are the same length because they are opposite sides.

50 ÷ 2 = 25
So a = 25 m and c = 25 m

You Can Work Out the Size of Missing Angles

Rectangles have equal angles. They are all right angles (90°).
You can use this information to work out the size of missing angles.

EXAMPLE: What is the size of angle v?

25° + v = 90°
So v = 90° − 25° = 65°

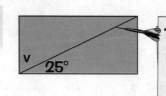

v   25°

This line is a diagonal line. It joins two corners that aren't next to each other.

"I can use my knowledge of rectangles to work out the length of missing sides and the size of missing angles."

Regular and Irregular Polygons

Regular Polygons Have Sides of Equal Length

A <u>polygon</u> is a <u>2D shape</u> with <u>straight sides</u>.
The <u>name</u> of a polygon tells you <u>how many sides and angles</u> it has.

Regular <u>pentagon</u>

<u>5</u> equal sides.
<u>5</u> equal angles.

Regular <u>hexagon</u>

<u>6</u> equal sides.
<u>6</u> equal angles.

Regular <u>heptagon</u>

<u>7</u> equal sides.
<u>7</u> equal angles.

Regular <u>octagon</u>

<u>8</u> equal sides.
<u>8</u> equal angles.

The Sides of Irregular Polygons Aren't Equal

These polygons are <u>irregular</u>.
Their sides are <u>not</u> all the same length.
Their angles are <u>not</u> all equal.

These are irregular octagons.
They each have 8 sides.

Regular or Irregular...?

| EXAMPLES: | Are these polygons <u>regular</u> or <u>irregular</u>? How do you know? |

This is a <u>regular</u> octagon.
Its <u>sides</u> are all <u>equal</u>.
Its <u>angles</u> are all <u>equal</u>.

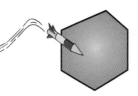

This is an <u>irregular</u> hexagon.
Its <u>sides</u> are <u>not all equal</u>.
Its <u>angles</u> are <u>not all equal</u>.

This is an <u>irregular</u> rectangle.
Its <u>angles</u> are <u>all equal</u> but
its sides are <u>not all equal</u>.

This is a <u>regular</u> pentagon.
Its <u>sides</u> are <u>all equal</u>.
Its <u>angles</u> are <u>all equal</u>.

"I can tell whether a polygon is regular or
irregular based on its sides and its angles."

 ✓ ✓   ✓

Reflection

Polygons Can be Symmetrical

This shape has a <u>mirror line</u>.
It is also called a <u>line of symmetry</u>.
If you put a mirror on that line, it looks
like you can see the <u>whole shape</u>.

Mirror line

All <u>regular polygons</u> have lines of symmetry.
Some irregular polygons do too.

Lines of symmetry: 3 1 0

Reflection in a Line

You can reflect shapes and patterns in a mirror line.

Each <u>point</u> and its <u>reflection</u> are exactly
the <u>same distance</u> from the mirror line.

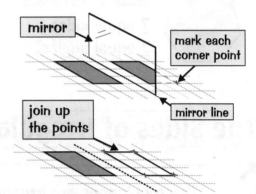

mirror

mark each corner point

mirror line

join up the points

EXAMPLE:

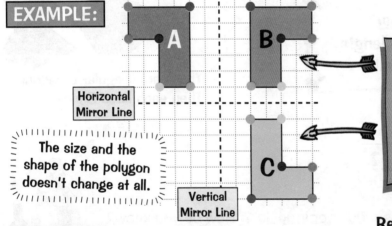

Horizontal Mirror Line

The size and the shape of the polygon doesn't change at all.

Vertical Mirror Line

B is the reflection of A in the <u>VERTICAL MIRROR LINE</u>.

C is the reflection of B in the <u>HORIZONTAL MIRROR LINE</u>.

EXAMPLE:

Shade in 9 more squares to
make this pattern symmetrical
in both mirror lines.

Reflect the pattern in <u>1 mirror line</u>... ...and <u>then</u> the other.

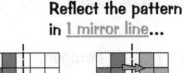

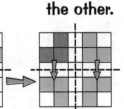

Tomas says, "Whichever of these two mirror lines
I reflect the arrow in, the direction of the arrow
will change." Is he correct? Explain your answer.

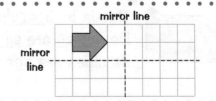

mirror line

mirror line

"I can draw where a shape will be after
it has been reflected in a mirror line."

Translation

Translation is Sliding

<u>Translation</u> sounds hard, but is <u>really easy</u>. It's when a shape <u>slides</u> from one place to another, <u>without</u> rotating or flipping over. The <u>size</u> and <u>shape</u> of it <u>doesn't change at all</u> — just its <u>position</u>.

EXAMPLE: Translate this shape 4 squares to the left.

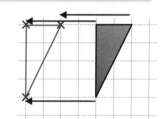

For <u>each vertex</u>, go 4 squares to the left and mark a cross. Then just <u>join up the crosses</u>.

SOME MORE EXAMPLES:

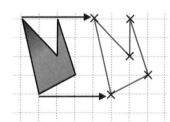

This is a translation 4 squares to the right.

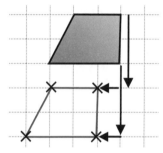

This is a translation 3 squares down and 1 square left.

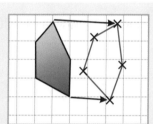

This is <u>not</u> a translation. The shape has <u>turned</u> as well as sliding.

Use Tracing Paper to Do Translations Easily

Put the tracing paper over the shape, trace it, and slide the tracing paper. Mark the vertices by pressing the point of your pencil through the tracing paper. Then take the tracing paper away and join up the vertices.

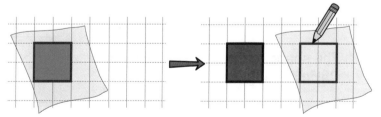

If you've got a <u>grid</u>, you can trace some of that too.

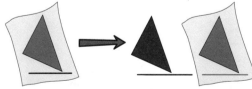

If you <u>haven't</u> got a grid, draw a <u>line</u> across on the original and the tracing paper. That way you can make sure you don't turn it.

"I can identify and draw where a shape will be after it has been translated. I can describe translations."

Practice Questions

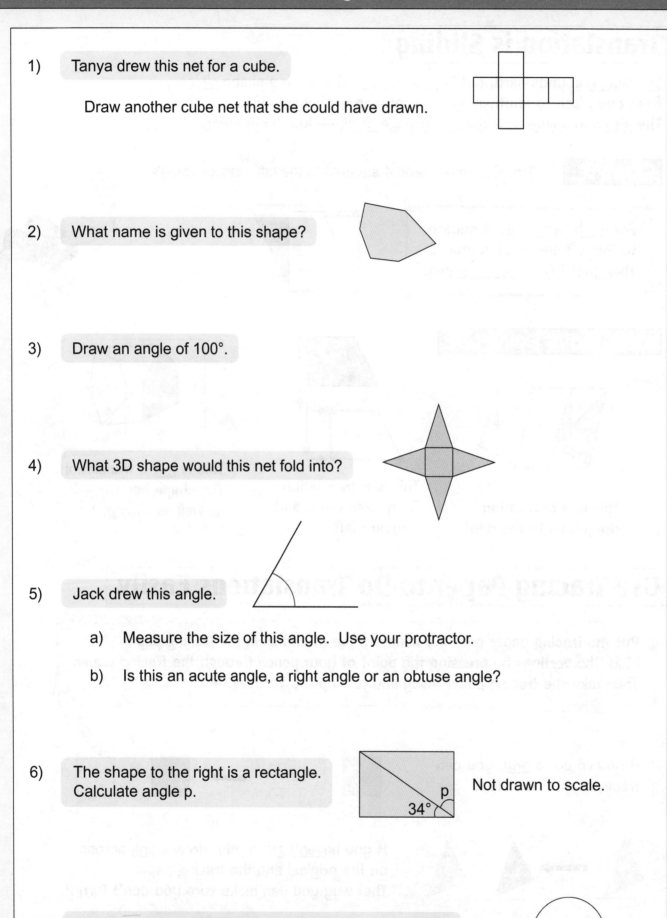

1)   Tanya drew this net for a cube.

Draw another cube net that she could have drawn.

2)   What name is given to this shape?

3)   Draw an angle of 100°.

4)   What 3D shape would this net fold into?

5)   Jack drew this angle.

a)   Measure the size of this angle. Use your protractor.

b)   Is this an acute angle, a right angle or an obtuse angle?

6)   The shape to the right is a rectangle.
Calculate angle p.

p

34°

Not drawn to scale.

7)   Estimate the size of this angle. Explain your reasoning.

Practice Questions

8) Copy this diagram.
Reflect the shape in both mirror lines.

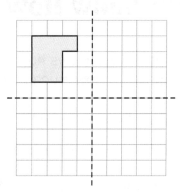

9) The shape on the right is a prism with a regular pentagon end.

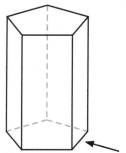

    a) Sketch the plan of the prism.

    b) Sketch the elevation of the prism from the direction of the arrow.

10) Shape A is translated 4 squares down and 4 squares right. Which shape does it end up on?

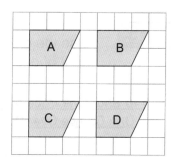

11) Calculate angle m.

Greater Depth

150°

m

Not drawn to scale.

12) The perimeter of this rectangle is 100 cm.
What are the lengths of the missing sides?

Greater Depth

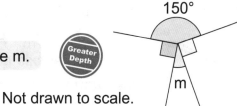

s

r   10 cm

t

13) The black line in this diagram is a straight line.
Calculate angle v.

Greater Depth

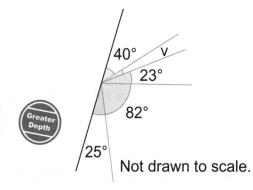

40°   v

23°

82°

25°

Not drawn to scale.

Section Five — Geometry

Line Graphs

Line Graphs Show How Something Changes

EXAMPLE:

The graph shows how the temperature on Faiza's island changed during the day. How much hotter was Faiza's island at 12:00 than at 14:00?

First, read both values from the graph.

① Find 12:00 on the horizontal axis and go straight up.

② When you reach the red line, go left to the vertical axis.

③ Read the value from the vertical axis.

④ Do the same for 14:00.

> 12:00 = 38 °C
> 14:00 = 28 °C

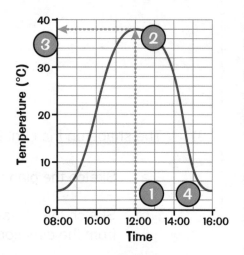

Then work out the difference by subtracting the smaller value from the larger one: 38 °C – 28 °C = 10 °C

So Faiza's island was 10 °C hotter at 12:00 than at 14:00.

EXAMPLE:

Use the graph below to find out the total cost of one apple and one orange in Week 2.

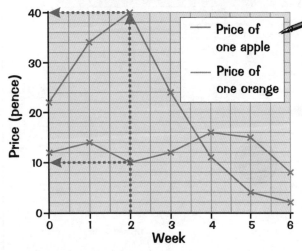

Graph to Show the Price of One Apple and One Orange Over Six Weeks

Key:
— Price of one apple
— Price of one orange

The key tells you what each line represents.

Find Week 2 on the horizontal axis and go straight up.

When you reach a coloured line, move across to the vertical axis to find the price of that item.

Apple = 40p   Orange = 10p

Add the values to get the total cost.

40 + 10 = 50p

So one apple and one orange would have cost 50p in Week 2.

Greater Depth

Lara wants to plot a graph comparing the amount of rainfall each month in Dryland and Wetland. The table on the right shows the total rainfall each month. Explain why she might find it difficult to plot both sets of data on the same graph.

Month	Wetland	Dryland
April	47 cm	0.4 cm
May	78 cm	0.2 cm
June	106 cm	0 cm

"I can solve problems using data from a line graph."

Tables and Timetables

Data Can be Organised in a Table

Tables are a handy way of <u>organising</u> and <u>presenting</u> data neatly.

EXAMPLE: Daima asks her sons how many carrots and how many potatoes they want with their Sunday roasts. Use the information below to complete the table.

Andrew wants two potatoes and three carrots. Michael only wants one carrot, but would like three times as many potatoes as Andrew. John wants four potatoes, and as many carrots as Michael and Andrew put together.

Name	Number of Potatoes	Number of Carrots
John	4	?
Andrew	2	3
Michael	?	1

John wants <u>as many</u> carrots as Michael and Andrew put together. Add together the values for Michael and Andrew: 3 + 1 = 4, so John wants <u>4 carrots</u>.

Michael wants <u>3 times</u> as many potatoes as Andrew. You're told that Andrew wants 2 potatoes, so <u>multiply</u>:

$$2 \times 3 = 6$$

Michael wants <u>6 potatoes</u>.

Name	Number of Potatoes	Number of Carrots
John	4	4
Andrew	2	3
Michael	6	1

Timetables Often Use the 24-Hour Clock

EXAMPLE: Betty has to get to Barrow by 3 o'clock.
What time is the latest train she can catch from Foxfield?

1) Look at the timetable. Each column gives you the times for one train.

2) Find <u>Barrow</u> in the timetable.

3) <u>Read along that row</u> until you find the last time before 3 o'clock (15:00). It's 14:59.

4) Then <u>read up that column</u> to the 'Foxfield' row. So the latest train Betty can get is the one at <u>14:38</u>.

Millom	12:57	14:28	14:59	16:23
Green Road	13:02	14:35	15:03	16:27
Foxfield	13:05	14:38	15:07	16:31
Kirkby	13:09	14:43	15:11	16:35
Askam	13:14	14:51	15:16	16:40
Barrow	13:27	14:59	15:29	16:53

"I can complete, read and interpret information in tables and timetables."

Practice Questions

1) A shopkeeper records how many jumpers she sells each month.

a) How many jumpers were sold in October?

b) In which month were the most jumpers sold?

c) How many jumpers were sold in total in July and August?

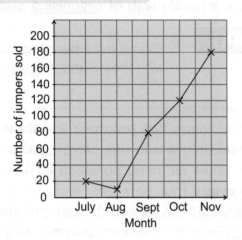

2) Joe organised an Easter egg hunt for his friends.
He made a table of how many eggs each person found.

	Number of eggs found
Max	12
Henry	7
Rex	15
Harold	4
Mavis	6

a) Who found the greatest number of eggs?

b) What was the lowest number of eggs found?

c) How many people found more than five eggs?

3) Jamie is baking a cake. The graph shows the temperature of the cake after he put it in the oven.

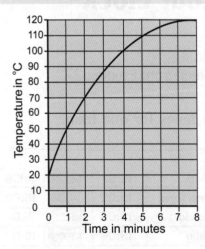

a) What was the temperature of the cake at 2 minutes?

b) After how many minutes did the cake reach 100 °C?

4) Anja ran herself a bath. The volume of the bath water increased by 8 litres every 30 seconds.

Copy and complete the table.

Time	Volume
30 secs	8 litres
60 secs	
90 secs	
120 secs	32 litres

Practice Questions

5) Janice is travelling by train from Sheffield to London.
The timetable is shown below.

Sheffield	0927	0959	1027	1059
Chesterfield	0938	1010	1038	1110
Derby	0959	1031	1059	1131
Leicester	1023	1055	1123	1155
London	1134	1208	1234	1308

a) How long does it take to travel between Derby and Leicester?

b) Janice needs to be in London by 12.30 pm. What time should she get on the train at Sheffield?

6) Clara works for a delivery company.
She is weighing and measuring the height of parcels.

Parcel A weighs 1.5 kg and is 20 cm tall.
Parcel B weighs 2.5 kg more than Parcel A. It is also three times taller.
Parcel C weighs 4 times more than Parcel B. It is 98 cm taller than Parcel A.

Put this information in a table.

7) The graph below shows the speeds of two cars during one lap of a race track.

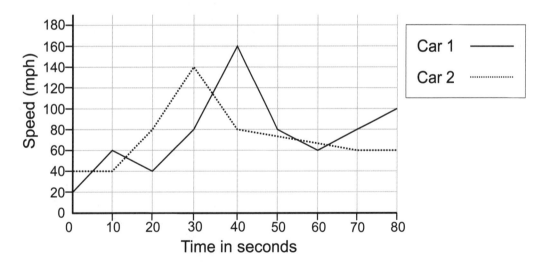

a) Which car was faster at 10 seconds?

b) How fast was Car 2 travelling when the speed of Car 1 was 20 mph?

c) How much faster was Car 1 travelling at 40 seconds than Car 2?

d) Which car spent longer above 80 mph?

Section Six — Statistics

Answers

Section One — Number and Place Value

Page 3 — Place Value in Big Numbers
Greater Depth: Any three sums that add to make
752 163. E.g. 750 000 + 2100 + 63
                      700 000 + 52 000 + 160 + 3
                      740 000 + 10 000 + 2100 + 60 + 3

Page 6 — Rounding
Greater Depth: To round to 20 000 to the nearest ten thousand, the number of computers sold in May must be between 15 000 and 24 999. To round to 25 000 to the nearest thousand, the number of computers sold in June must be between 24 500 and 25 499. If the number of computers sold in June is between 24 500 and 24 999, Jia might not be correct.

Pages 8-9 — Practice Questions
1)   a) −7
      b) 5
      c) −7
      You could use a number line to help you.
2)   a) −7 < 4
      b) −5 > −9
3)   a) 800 000
      b) 845 000
      c) 845 330
4)   a) 4 million
      b) 2 hundred thousand
      c) 5 thousand
5)   a) 1 440 563
      b) 907 244
6)   22 100, 22 504, 22 567, 23 176
7)   52 259, 51 259, 50 259
8)   −9 °C (or a decrease of 9 °C)
9)   a) −3 °C
      b) 20 °C
10)   570
      D = 500, L = 50, XX = 20, so DLXX is
      500 + 50 + 20 = 570.
11)   a) the Ice Cream Party
      b) 565 000
      c) 560 000
12)   1991
13)   a) 3467
      b) 3600
         The population of Bringantum is 3637.
      c) Hillsius, Ulverstiun, Roundle, Brigantum
         In order, the populations are:
         2949, 3424, 3467, 3637.

Section Two — Calculations

Page 13 — Rounding and Checking
Greater Depth: When doing the inverse calculations, he has rounded up the numbers that are added, and rounded down the number that is subtracted, so the estimate will be more than the actual score.

Page 17 — Factors and Primes
Greater Depth: The prime factors of 35 are 5 and 7, so you need to find the next age Mia will be that has one of these numbers as a prime factor. E.g.
$36 = 9 \times 4 = 9 \times 2 \times 2$, so it's not 36.
37 is a prime number, so it's not 37.
$38 = 19 \times 2$, so it's not 38.
$39 = 13 \times 3$, so it's not 39.
$40 = 10 \times 4 = 5 \times 2 \times 2 \times 2$, so it is **40**.
You could also work out that the next number which has 5 or 7 as a factor must be either 5 or 7 more than 35.
$35 + 5 = 40$ and $35 + 7 = 42$, so it is 40.

Page 23 — Solving Calculation Problems
Greater Depth: E.g. method 1: $1180 − 220 = 960$.
$960 \div 120 = 8$, so he's had the dinosaur for 8 days.
Method 2: count the number of steps of 120 it takes to get from 220 to 1180 — (220), 340, 460, 580, 700, 820, 940, 1060, 1180 = 8 steps, so he's had the dinosaur for 8 days.

Pages 24-25 — Practice Questions
1)
$$\begin{array}{r} 1\,359 \\ +\,8\,472 \\ \hline 9\,831 \\ \hline {\scriptstyle 1\,1} \end{array}$$

2)   49.73 rounds up to 50.
      92.21 rounds down to 90.
      $50 + 90 = \mathbf{140}$. This is close to Jenny's answer, so it is likely to be **right**.
3)   5, 10, 15, 20, 25 and 30.
      Multiples of 5 are just numbers in the 5 times table.
4)   Yes, 23 is a prime number.
5)
$$\begin{array}{r} 2\,381 \\ +\,1\,556 \\ \hline 3\,937 \end{array}$$

6)
$$\begin{array}{r} \cancel{8}\overset{7}{}\,\cancel{1}\overset{15}{}\,\cancel{6}\overset{5}{}\,5 \\ -\,5\,329 \\ \hline 2\,836 \end{array}$$

7)   1 and 48, 2 and 24, 3 and 16, 4 and 12, 6 and 8.
8)   The factors of 12 are 1, 2, 3, 4, 6 and 12.
      The factors of 18 are 1, 2, 3, 6, 9 and 18.
      The factors of 40 are 1, 2, 4, 5, 8, 10, 20 and 40.
      So their common factors are **1 and 2**.
      Common factors are factors that the numbers share.
9) $9 \times 9 = \mathbf{81}$
10)   a) $4.35 \times 1000 = \mathbf{4350}$
      b) $26 \div 100 = \mathbf{0.26}$
11)   a) 11 228 + 2400
        = 11 000 + 200 + 28 + 2000 + 400
        = 13 000 + 200 + 28 + 400
        = 13 000 + 600 + 28 = **13 628**
      b) 8820 − 2100 = 8820 − 2000 − 100
        = 6820 − 100 = **6720**

12) a) 9 into 75 goes 8 times with remainder 3.
So Micky can buy **8 bags** (and has 3p left).

b) 6 into 16 goes 2 times with remainder 4.
2 bags is only 12 frog legs, so you have to
round your answer up to **3**.

13) a) E.g. Split 12 into its factors, 3 and 4.
$300 \div 3 = 100$
$100 \div 4 = 25$
So $300 \div 12 = \textbf{25}$

b) E.g. Work out 100×7 then add on 3×7.
$100 \times 7 = 700$
$3 \times 7 = 21$
$700 + 21 = \textbf{721}$

14) a) $5^2 = 5 \times 5 = \textbf{25}$

b) $3^3 = 3 \times 3 \times 3 = 9 \times 3 = 27$
$27 - 25 = \textbf{2}$

15) $6 \times 3 = 9 \times \square$
$18 = 9 \times \square$
$9 \times 2 = 18$, so one sausage costs **£2**.

16)
```
      1 2 6
9 |1¹1²3 ⁵4
```
So there's **126 g** of cheese in one pie.

17) a) His estimate will be higher than the actual
amount as he has rounded both numbers up.

b)
```
      1 4 2 2
    ×     1 7
    ---------
      9 9 5 4
  + 1 4 2 2 0
    ---------
    2 4 1 7 4
```
So Sam needs **24 174 mm** of fabric.

18) a) E.g. $15 = 5 \times 3$
$60 \div 5 = 12$
$12 \div 3 = 4$. So it takes her **4 minutes**.
You need to do $60 \div 15$, so make it easier by
splitting 15 into two factors (5×3) and dividing
first by 5 and then by 3.

b) E.g. 15 is the same as $10 + 5$.
$60 \times 10 = 600$. Then add 60×5.
You know $6 \times 5 = 30$, so you also know that
$60 \times 5 = 300$.
So $60 \times 15 = 600 + 300 = \textbf{900 boxes}$.
You need to do 15×60, so make an easier
calculation first and then adjust.

Section 3 — Fractions, Decimals and Percentages

Page 27 — Equivalent Fractions
Greater Depth: $\frac{1}{5} = \frac{3}{15} = \frac{5}{25}$

Page 31 — Multiplying with Fractions
Greater Depth: She has done the calculations the
wrong way round — she should have multiplied by 6
and then divided by 12, to get $4 \times 6 = 24$, $24 \div 12 = \textbf{2}$.

Page 33 — Rounding Decimals
Greater Depth 1: 3.49 rounds down to 3.

Greater Depth 2: 10 numbers: 1.55, 1.56, 1.57, 1.58,
1.59, 1.60, 1.61, 1.62, 1.63, 1.64

Page 36 — Percentages, Fractions and Decimals

Greater Depth 1: E.g. $\frac{2}{5}, \frac{4}{10}, \frac{6}{15}, \frac{8}{20}$

Greater Depth 2: $\frac{13}{20} = \frac{65}{100} = 0.65$, so e.g. **0.7** is bigger
than 0.65 and **0.6** is smaller than 0.65.

Pages 38-39 — Practice Questions

1) $\frac{13}{1000}$

2) a) $\frac{27}{100}$

b) $\frac{91}{100}$

c) $\frac{3}{100}$

3) 8

4) 0.05, 0.056, 0.223, 0.227, 1.01

5) $\frac{7}{4} = \frac{4}{4} + \frac{3}{4} = 1\frac{3}{4}$

6) 0.4

7) $\frac{6}{10}$
To find an equivalent fraction, multiply or divide
the top and bottom of the fraction by the same
number.

8) E.g. 16 and 8 are both multiples of 4, so find
equivalent fractions with 4 as the denominator.
$\frac{12}{16} = \frac{3}{4}, \frac{2}{8} = \frac{1}{4}$
So the order from smallest to largest is $\frac{2}{8}, \frac{2}{4}, \frac{12}{16}$
You can find equivalent fractions using a
different denominator as long as you make sure
that all the denominators are the same.

9) E.g. $\frac{6}{25} = \frac{24}{100} = 24\%$
So **Freddie** won the larger percentage of races.
You could also work this out by converting 28% to
a fraction and $\frac{6}{25}$ to hundredths.
When both amounts are fractions with the same
denominator, you can compare the numerators.

10) a) $\frac{2}{5} = \frac{4}{10}$
$\frac{4}{10} + \frac{9}{10} = \frac{13}{10} = \frac{10}{10} + \frac{3}{10} = 1\frac{3}{10}$

b) $5 \times 12 = 60$
$60 \div 7 = 8$ remainder $4 = 8\frac{4}{7}$

c) $2\frac{5}{12} = \frac{12}{12} + \frac{12}{12} + \frac{5}{12} = \frac{29}{12}$
$\frac{5}{6} = \frac{10}{12}$
$\frac{29}{12} - \frac{10}{12} = \frac{19}{12} = \frac{12}{12} + \frac{7}{12} = 1\frac{7}{12}$

11) You want to find $\frac{2}{3}$ of 18.
$18 \div 3 = 6$
$2 \times 6 = \textbf{12 cakes}$

12)
```
  ⁴5¹²3.⁹0̶¹0
  - 2 6.9 9
  ----------
    2 6.0 1
```
So she has **£26.01** left.

13) a) $\frac{12}{25} = \frac{48}{100} = \textbf{48\%}$

b) $\frac{7}{10} = \frac{70}{100} = \textbf{70\%}$

c) $0.51 \times 100 = \textbf{51\%}$

14) 14 out of 50 as a fraction is $\frac{14}{50}$.

To convert to a percentage, make an equivalent fraction with 100 as the denominator:

$\frac{14}{50} = \frac{28}{100} = \textbf{28\%}$

15) $15\% = \frac{15}{100}$, so you need to find $\frac{15}{100}$ of 200.

$200 \div 100 = 2$. $2 \times 15 = 30$ sweets.

So the number of sweets he has left is:

$200 - 30 = \textbf{170}$

16) a) You need to find equivalent fractions of $\frac{1}{4}$ and $\frac{2}{5}$ that have a common denominator.

For example, you could use 20 as the common denominator.

Hassan has eaten: $\frac{2}{5} = \frac{8}{20}$ of the bar

Sally eats: $\frac{1}{4} = \frac{5}{20}$ of the bar

$\frac{8}{20} - \frac{5}{20} = \frac{3}{20}$

So Hassan has eaten $\frac{\textbf{3}}{\textbf{20}}$ more of the bar.

b) Total fraction eaten: $\frac{8}{20} + \frac{5}{20} = \frac{13}{20}$

The mass of chocolate they've eaten is

$\frac{13}{20} \times 100$ g.

$100 \div 20 = 5$

$13 \times 5 = 65$ g

So the mass of chocolate left is:

$100 - 65 = \textbf{35 g}$.

Section Four — Measurement

Page 41 — Imperial Units

Greater Depth: 4 ounces ≈ 100 g, so 8 ounces ≈ 200 g. 1000 g = 1 kg, so 200 g = 200 ÷ 1000 = **0.2 kg**.

Page 44 — Area

Greater Depth: Keziah has counted every square that the shape touches, rather than counting the whole squares and estimating using the squares that are more than half covered. Keziah hasn't looked at the size of the squares in the grid, and has assumed each square is 1 cm², instead of 100 cm².

Pages 50-51 — Practice Questions

1) 1 kg = 1000 g
So 3.4 kg = 3.4 × 1000 = **3400 g**

2) 1 km = 1000 m
So 2600 m = 2600 ÷ 1000 = **2.6 km**

3) 1 week = 7 days
So 15 ÷ 7 = 2 remainder 1, so Sarah went on holiday for **2 weeks and 1 day**.

4) Perimeter = 6 + 11 + 6 + 11 = **34 m**

5) Area = 3 × 4 = **12 m²**

6) 19 squares are more than half covered. Each square is 1 cm². So the area of the shape is around **19 cm²**.

7) The shape is made up of 11 cubes. Each cube is 1 cm³ so the volume of the shape is **11 cm³**.

8) a) 1 kg ≈ 2 lbs
So 4 kg = 4 × 2 = 8 lbs
So **4 kg is bigger** than 6 lbs.

b) 1 l = 1000 ml
So 16.5 l = 16.5 × 1000 = 16 500 ml
So **16.5 l is bigger** than 1650 ml.

c) 1 l ≈ 2 pints
So 18 l = 18 × 2 = 36 pints
So **18 l is bigger** than 30 pints.

9) Shaun drinks 4 × 300 ml = 1200 ml.
2 l × 1000 = 2000 ml
So there's 2000 − 1200 = **800 ml left**.
You need to make sure that all the measurements are in the same units in your calculations.

10) Find the missing measurements:
2 + 2 = 4 cm.
3 − 1 = 2 cm.
Perimeter = 3 + 4 + 1 + 2 + 2 + 2 = **14 cm**

11) Perimeter = 20 + 15 + 20 + 15 = 70 m
So Arthur **will not** have enough fencing.
Rectangles have two pairs of equal sides, so you can work out from the question that two sides will be 20 metres and the other two will be 15 metres.

12) Area of garden = 4 × 5 = 20 m²
Area of pond = 2 × 3 = 6 m²
So the area of the garden that surrounds the pond is 20 − 6 = **14 m²**

13) Perimeter = 6 + x + 6 + x = 22

So 12 + 2x = 22
Get x on its own:
2x = 22 − 12
2x = 10
Then divide by 2 to get x on its own:
x = 10 ÷ 2
x = 5
So the rectangle has a width of **5 cm**.
You can use 'x' for any number you don't know.

Section Five — Geometry

Page 54 — Angles

Greater Depth 1: Angle x is smaller than a right angle, which is 90°. 100° is bigger than 90°, so Emi's measurement must be incorrect.

Greater Depth 2: E.g. she might have read from the wrong scale (the one that doesn't start from 0° on the line of the angle).

Page 56 — Angle Rules

Greater Depth: Angles that meet on a straight line add up to 180°. 180° − 50° = 130°, so the two remaining angles must add up to 130°. They could be, e.g. **70°** and **60°**.

Page 60 — Reflection

Greater Depth: He is **incorrect**. Reflecting in the vertical mirror line will make the arrow point in the opposite direction, but reflecting in the horizontal line will not change the direction of the arrow.

Pages 62-63 — Practice Questions

1) E.g.

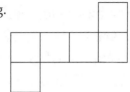

Any set of 6 squares that can be folded into a cube is correct.

2) An irregular hexagon
3)

4) (Square-based) pyramid
5) a) 60°
   b) an acute angle
      60° is less than 90° (a right angle) so it's an acute angle.
6) 34° + p = 90°
   So p = 90° − 34°
   p = 56°
7) This angle is a bit less than 180°.
   So a good estimate would be **170°**.
8)

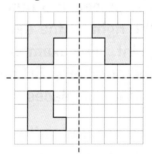

9) a) Plan:

   b) Elevation:

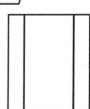

10) shape D
11) 150° + 90° + 90° + m = 360°
    So m = 360° − 150° − 90° − 90°
    m = 30°
12) **r = 10 cm** because the opposite side is 10 cm.
    So 10 + 10 + s + t = 100
    s + t = 100 − 10 − 10
    s + t = 80
    s and t are the same length because they are opposite sides.
    80 ÷ 2 = 40
    So **s = 40 cm** and **t = 40 cm**

13) 40° + 25° + 82° + 23° + v = 180°
    So v = 180° − 40° − 25° − 82° − 23°
    v = 10°
    These angles meet on a straight line so they must add up to 180°.

Section Six — Statistics

Page 64 — Line Graphs

Greater Depth: The amount of rainfall is much bigger in Wetland than in Dryland, so it will be hard to find a sensible scale that you can accurately plot both sets of data on.

Pages 66-67 — Practice Questions

1) a) 120
   b) November
   c) July = 20
      August = 10
      20 + 10 = 30
      So **30 jumpers** were sold in July and August.
2) a) Rex
   b) 4 eggs
   c) 4 people
3) a) 70 °C
   b) 4 minutes
4)

Time	Volume
30 secs	8 litres
60 secs	16 litres
90 secs	24 litres
120 secs	32 litres

5) a) 24 minutes
   b) 0959
6) E.g.

	Weight (kg)	Height (cm)
Parcel A	1.5	20
Parcel B	1.5 + 2.5 = **4**	20 × 3 = **60**
Parcel C	4 × 4 = **16**	20 + 98 = **118**

7) a) Car 1
   b) 40 mph
   c) Speed of Car 1 = 160 mph
      Speed of Car 2 = 80 mph
      160 − 80 = 80
      So Car 1 was **80 mph** faster.
   d) Car 1 was above 80 mph between 30 and 50 seconds. 50 − 30 = 20 seconds.
      Car 1 was also above 80 mph between 70 and 80 seconds. 80 − 70 = 10 seconds.
      So Car 1 was above 80 mph for 30 seconds in total.
      Car 2 was above 80 mph between 20 and 40 seconds. 40 − 20 = 20 seconds.
      So **Car 1** spent longer above 80 mph.
      Look at the graph carefully for Car 1 — there are two different times when it is travelling above 80 mph.

Glossary

2D	2D is short for two-dimensional. It means flat.
3D	3D is short for three-dimensional. A 3D shape is just the same as a solid shape.
acute angles	Angles that are less than a $\frac{1}{4}$ turn (90°). They are smaller than right angles.
area	The area of a shape is the amount of surface it covers.
ascending	Getting higher. Ascending order means from smaller to bigger.
axis/axes	The horizontal axis is the line along the bottom of a graph or chart. The vertical axis is the line up the left-hand side. Axes is the word for more than one axis.
capacity	The amount something can hold when it's full. Capacity is often measured in litres or millilitres.
common factor	Factors which two or more numbers share. For example, the factors of 6 are 1, 2, 3 and 6. The factors of 9 are 1, 3 and 9. So 3 is a common factor of 6 and 9.
common multiple	Multiples which two or more numbers share. For example, multiples of 3 are 3, 6, 9, 12, 15... Multiples of 5 are 5, 10, 15... 15 is a common multiple of 3 and 5.
cube number	The result of multiplying a number by itself twice. For example, $3 \times 3 \times 3 = 27$, so 27 is a cube number.
cubic centimetre, cm³	A unit for measuring volume. A cube with sides 1 cm long.
data	Data is just information.
decimal places	The places in a number to the right of the decimal point. For example, the number 4.56 has 2 decimal places.
decimal point	The dot you write in a decimal number. It comes between the ones and the tenths.
degrees, °	The units used to measure angles. For example, a right angle measures 90°.
denominator	The bottom number of a fraction.
descending	Getting lower. Descending order means from bigger to smaller.
difference	How much bigger one number is than another.

Glossary

elevation — The view of an object from one side. Elevations can also be called projections.

equivalent — Something that has the same value. For example, $\frac{1}{2}$ and $\frac{2}{4}$ are equivalent fractions.

estimate — An estimate is a sensible guess at the answer. You can use rounding to help you estimate answers.

face — A side of a solid shape. Faces can be flat, as on cubes. They can also be curved, as on cylinders.

factor — A factor of a number is a whole number that divides exactly into that number. For example, the factors of 6 are 1, 2, 3 and 6.

hundredths — The second digit after the decimal point. One hundredth is written 0.01 or $\frac{1}{100}$.

imperial units — These are old units for measuring distance, mass and capacity. Imperial distance units include miles, yards, feet and inches. Imperial mass units include pounds and ounces. Imperial capacity units include pints.

improper fraction — A fraction with a numerator bigger than its denominator, for example $\frac{9}{7}$.

inverse — Opposite. For example, addition and subtraction are inverse operations.

irregular polygon — In an irregular polygon, not all sides are of equal length and/or not all of the angles are equal.

line of symmetry — If you put a mirror on the line of symmetry, it looks like you can see the whole shape.

mass — Mass is what most people mean when they say 'weight'. A brick has a greater mass than a loaf of bread. Mass is measured in grams or kilograms.

metric units — These are the modern units for measuring distance, mass and capacity. Metric distance units include mm, cm, m and km. Metric mass units include g and kg. Metric capacity units include ml and l.

mirror line — The same as a line of symmetry.

mixed number — A mixed number has a whole-number part and a fraction part, for example $3\frac{1}{10}$.

Glossary

multiple	Multiples are the numbers in a times table, e.g. multiples of 6 are 6, 12, 18,... They go on forever, because you can always multiply by higher numbers.
negative	Negative numbers are numbers less than 0. For example, –1 or –10.
net	A 2D shape that will fold up to make a 3D shape.
numerator	The top number of a fraction.
obtuse angles	Angles that are between a $\frac{1}{4}$ turn (90°) and a $\frac{1}{2}$ turn (180°). They're bigger than right angles.
ordering	Putting in order. For example, to order 3, 1 and 2 from smallest to largest, start with the smallest, then the next smallest: 1, 2, 3.
parallel	Parallel lines are straight lines that are always the same distance apart and never meet or cross.
partition	Split a number up. You can partition numbers in many ways. For example, 173 = 100 + 70 + 3 or 173 = 150 + 20 + 3
perimeter	The total distance around the outside of a shape.

plan	The view of an object from directly above.
polygon	A 2D (flat) shape with straight sides.
powers of 10	Numbers that are a 1 followed by just zeros: 10, 100, 1000, 10 000, 100 000 and 1 000 000 are powers of 10.
prime factor	A factor of a number that is also a prime number. For example, the prime factors of 20 are 5 and 2.
prime number	A number that has exactly two factors: 1 and itself. For example, 2, 3, 5, 7, etc.
projection	The view of an object from one side. Projections can also be called elevations.
proper fraction	A fraction that's less than 1. The numerator is smaller than the denominator. For example, $\frac{2}{5}$ or $\frac{3}{4}$.
protractor	You can use a protractor to measure angles.
rectangle	A flat shape with 4 sides. It has 2 pairs of equal sides and 4 right angles.
reflection	A reflection of a shape is a mirror image.

Glossary

reflex angle	Angles that are more than a $\frac{1}{2}$ turn (180°).
regular polygon	In a regular polygon, all the sides are equal lengths and all the angles are the same.
remainder	What's left over when you divide. For example, $7 \div 2 = 3$ remainder 1.
right angle	A quarter turn, or 90°.
Roman numerals	Letters that the Romans used to show numbers, before the digits 0-9 were invented. For example, $V = 5$ and $X = 10$.
rounding	Finding a nearby number that's similar, but easier to use in calculations. For example, to round 27 to the nearest 10, you have to find the number that's nearest to 27 and a multiple of 10. 27 is between 20 and 30 but nearer to 30.
square centimetre, cm²	A unit for measuring area. A square with sides 1 cm long.
square number	The result of multiplying a number by itself. For example, $2 \times 2 = 4$, $3 \times 3 = 9$. 4 and 9 are both square numbers.
tenths	The first digit after the decimal point. One tenth is written 0.1 or $\frac{1}{10}$.
thousandths	The third digit after the decimal point. One thousandth is written 0.001 or $\frac{1}{1000}$.
translation	When a shape slides from one place to another without rotating or flipping.
vertex/ vertices	A vertex is a corner. Vertices is the word for corners.
volume	The volume of a shape is the amount of space it takes up.
weight	How heavy something is. Usually when people say weight, they mean mass (how many grams or kilograms there are). Weight and mass are different. Don't worry about it though. It's quite hard and you don't have to understand it just yet.

Index